High Trip, ca. 1930. Photograph by Cedric Wright.

NORMAN CLYDE *of the* SIERRA NEVADA

Dear Dave:

By coincidence, your letter from Alaska asking me about Norman arrived the same day we went to Big Pine to see him. He is in the Sanitorium there, with a little flu and on top of that his leg is acting up again and he couldn't walk very well. He had a grocery box of books brought down from the Baker Creek cabin, and was churning through Goethe in German, with a six-inch thick dictionary which he picked up at a rummage sale in Bishop, and a New Testament in Portuguese which he bought for Spanish but was reading anyway. On his night stand was a Life of Napoleon *in French, which he has already read three times.*

He is just about recovered and looks very well because the hospital holds back on his potatoes and he trims down a bit. "These places like to keep a man in, to make sure he doesn't have a relapse, and they have their regulations but I've got a lot of chores to do up there, there's wood to cut . . . "

Nonesense. He has wood for several seasons and the rest and relief from doing everything for himself is good for him.

————————◆————————

We camped on a little snow-free patch of rock on the frozen lake in the Palisades that early-season trip long ago. I can still remember my awe at the collection of gear Norman drew out of his duffle bag. There's part of the weight right there. The duffle bag was lashed to a six-pound Yukon pack frame which also supported a full length Hudson Bay axe. But perhaps the kitchen bag was the most surprising to Hubert and me, as our meager assortment of pans scrounged from depression cupboards was no match for Norman's six large kettles, the cups and spoons, the dishes and bowls, the salt shakers, condiments, servers and graters and, for all I know, cookie cutters. I can remember my astonishment at seeing his special stick-mop for washing dishes. And he even had extra food for us! Bob Clunie would never believe it, because Norman used to drop in at that well-supplied artist's camp with great frequency and famous appetite.

Perhaps the duplications in Norman's list contrasted most strongly with our Boy Scout style. Boots? He carried several; ski boots, tricouni boots, rubber-soled boots for the rocks, camp slippers. "It's not true that I carry an anvil in my pack. Only this little piece of iron to put in the heel for replacing tricounis. That's something these go-lightly boys never think about. Some gaffer is always tearing out some nails and needing repairs. And anyway, if I want to carry a rock in my pack to keep me steady down the trail, that's my business."

A camera? Norman carried five. That's right. A 35mm loaded with Ansco and one with Eastman film, a 120 for black and white and another 120 for color, and of course his "throw-in-the-lake" camera, which was the spare.

A book for evening reading? Well, Norman usually travels alone and on long trips, so he had a rather large library in many languages. "They last longer, especially the Greek as I'm usually a little rusty in that." And a pistola, or maybe several in different calibers and types. Evenings on the trip we watched him throw chips from the woodpile out on the ice and shoot at them. If hit dead center the chip would scoot across the lake without spinning. If he hit a chip and made it twirl, he would mutter angrily.

We weighed one of those loads once. Norman showed up at the house around 1950, complaining of losing track of the days. It seemed his stick-notching was inaccurate or something, and he was a day late meeting Jules Eichorn and his party, for a month's cache and carry trip. I mention cache and carry because Jules had already deposited food along the route, and Norman's pack contained only five pounds of edibles for emergency. Still the pack weighed out at ninety-two pounds. We divided it into four loads and carried to Paiute Pass to help Norman catch up with Jules. At the pass, we lashed the whole mess to the Yukon board, along with two fishing rods (eight-foot for streams, nine-foot for lakes), reels and a spare reel. Away he went.

He caught up with the party all right, but did not come out again for six weeks. When he was two weeks overdue, we began to worry, and went to Independence to check on him, but there he was coming out over Kearsarge Pass with a pack which went to one hundred six pounds. The surplus was accounted for by pots and pans he scrounged along the way, and food he purchased at Giant Forest and a string of fish.

You asked me to write some memories of my trips with Norman, and I seem to have gotten stuck on his packs. There's lots more I could tell as one recollection triggers another, and even some more stories of the packs come to mind. I think many people might find his way of travel in the mountains quite strange, especially with today's gear but, you see, Norman was not just visiting the mountains or passing through the peaks. He lived there . . .

Fourth Recess, August 8, 1970

NORMAN CLYDE
of the
SIERRA NEVADA

Rambles Through the Range of Light

29 Essays on the Mountains
by Norman Clyde

Foreword by Francis Farquhar

Prologue by Jules Eichorn

with a long letter from Smoke Blanchard

15 photographs
of the Old Gaffer

SCRIMSHAW PRESS 1971

Library of Congress Catalog Card Number 71-183953.
ISBN 0-912020-19-9 paper,
0-912020-20-2 cloth.

Publication number eleven by the Press
149 9th Street, San Francisco 94103.

Foreword

I FIRST MET Norman Clyde in 1920 on a climb of the North Palisade. I was making the ascent on the usual route with Will Colby and Walter Huber. We were nearing the top when we heard someone coming behind us. The climber overtook us and turned out to be Clyde, who had been at the Sierra Club camp at Simpson Meadow. He had heard that we were making the climb and set out to join us. He was his usual extraordinary self, carrying a pack and a cartridge belt and a revolver. What the latter two were for is hard to conceive.

I am sure not many people realize what an amazing character Clyde is. His mountain exploits are well known, for he has climbed an incredible number of peaks both in the United States and Canada. But I doubt if many know his intellectual achievements. Not only was he a graduate of Geneva College at Beaver Falls, Pennsylvania, but he also holds an honorary degree of Doctor of Science from Geneva. At one time he studied Old English at Berkeley, and he has the qualifications for a teacher in the California school system.

Above all this Clyde was a man of great kindness. Time and again he went out of his way to rescue people in trouble in the mountains.

For many years Norman has supported himself by writing articles about his climbs and the following compilation will, I am sure, be well received not only by his many friends but by a much wider audience.

FRANCIS P. FARQUHAR
Berkeley
December 1970

Prologue

WHEN I FIRST HEARD OF Norman Clyde, he was already a legendary figure. He had climbed solo almost all the important peaks of the Sierra Nevada, rescued numerous lost souls, located crashed airplanes, and carried a pack so heavy only he could handle it. I therefore had a strong desire to meet this superhuman person, and the chance came in the summer of 1931.

Through the efforts of Francis Farquhar, then Vice-President of the Sierra Club, Robert Underhill was enticed to come west and climb in the Sierra, with the idea of making some new routes and first ascents as well as demonstrating the proper use and management of the rope. Clyde was to be a part of the climbing team, which included my favorite climbing partner of the early thirties, Glen Dawson.

I first saw Clyde standing in the sun in front of Glacier Lodge, a jut-jawed, blue-eyed, ruddy complexioned, animated block of granite, somewhat resembling a soldier—mainly, I think, because of his campaign hat, which never (as I learned) left his head. My impression was that here was a man who had made up his mind what he had to do and would never swerve from his objectives. But, I asked myself, "How could a man with a build like Norman's be such a good mountain climber?" I was soon to find out. Immediate objectives for the group were to be a new route on Temple Crag, a traverse from North Palisade north to the second highest point, and the northwest peak of the North Palisade, which was unclimbed and later received the name "Thunderbolt Peak" because of the events which subsequently took place.

On the Thunderbolt Peak climb, where all of us almost lost our lives because of the suddenness of a thunderstorm, Norman proved to be the most remarkable of mountaineers. In weather conditions which included lightning, snow, hail, sleet and rain, plus zero visibility, he got us safely off the peak and down the east face of the crest, where we roped into the bergschrund in total darkness. Then across the heavily crevassed Palisade Glacier to camp, arriving around midnight. This tour de force made me realize how great Norman's mountaineering ability was.

Another instance, although a less critical situation, was the mild trip prior to the first ascent of the east face of Mt. Whitney, mild because of Norman's uncanny ability to find the easiest route from Whitney Portals to East Face Lake. Not only did all the ledges connect but on them were patches of ripe, juicy currants, just as Norman predicted.

For a few years after the Whitney climb I had little mountain contact with Norman, but in the forties and fifties we renewed our association. These were the years when I would plan a month's backpacking trip in the Sierra with twelve to fifteen boys. I always had one assistant and whenever possible Norman was with me. It was on these numerous trips that the great breadth of the man became more and more apparent. He carried in his mind the geology, botany, wildlife and other interrelated information of the Sierra. His ability to handle an axe, fly rod or pistola was extraordinary. And his tremendous pack contained not only a complete commissary kit, assorted nails, wire, extra boots, throw-in-the-lake cameras (at one time I counted five) and many other various and sundry articles, but books of poetry and prose from the greatest classical authors in original German, French, Spanish, Italian, and sometimes English. None but Norman Clyde could possibly fit such a description.

Two more things especially impressed me about Norman. One was his huge appetite and the other his volatile temper, which flared up like Old Faithful when the occasion warranted. I shall never forget a certain breakfast when we were camped in Dusy Basin at the end of a month's trip. I was trying to finish up some hot cake batter and Norman was in his usual eating position, lying on the ground with his left arm propping up his body and holding out an empty plate. After he had consumed about forty six-inch cakes I asked, "Norman, how about a few more?" His classical, drawling answer was, "Well . . . all right!"

Although Norman was not known as a conservationist he very quietly did his thing. He made his mark in the world of mountains, but did not disturb them in doing so. To sum up, for me there can never be another human being so completely in tune with his chosen environment—the mountains— as Norman Clyde.

JULES EICHORN
Echo Lake
April 1971

"After a toilsome climb on the 10th of July up the rough abandoned trail over Harrison Pass at an elevation of 12,000 feet
above the sea, I set down my heavy pack and looked about for
a mountain to climb."

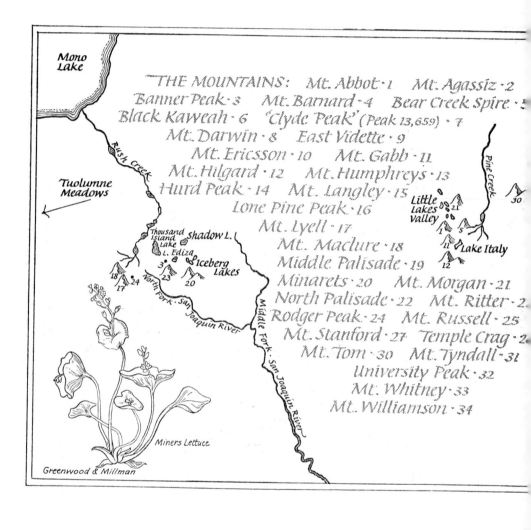

Mono Lake

Rush Creek

Tuolumne Meadows

THE MOUNTAINS: Mt. Abbot · 1   Mt. Agassiz · 2
Banner Peak · 3   Mt. Barnard · 4   Bear Creek Spire · 5
Black Kaweah · 6   'Clyde Peak' (Peak 13,659) · 7
Mt. Darwin · 8   East Vidette · 9
Mt. Ericsson · 10   Mt. Gabb · 11
Mt. Hilgard · 12   Mt. Humphreys · 13
Hurd Peak · 14   Mt. Langley · 15
Lone Pine Peak · 16
Mt. Lyell · 17
Mt. Maclure · 18
Middle Palisade · 19
Minarets · 20   Mt. Morgan · 21
North Palisade · 22   Mt. Ritter · 23
Rodger Peak · 24   Mt. Russell · 25
Mt. Stanford · 27   Temple Crag · 28
Mt. Tom · 30   Mt. Tyndall · 31
University Peak · 32
Mt. Whitney · 33
Mt. Williamson · 34

Pine Creek

Little Lakes Valley

Lake Italy

Thousand Island Lake   Shadow L.
L. Ediza
Iceberg Lakes

North Fork · San Joaquin River

Middle Fork · San Joaquin River

Miners Lettuce

Greenwood & Millman

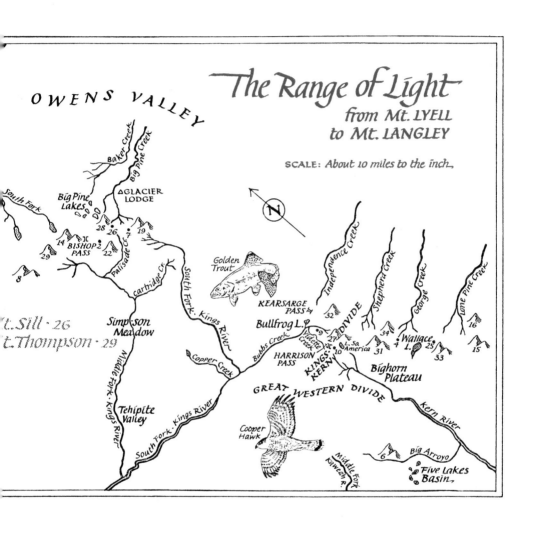

The First Ascent of the Highest of the Minarets [Clyde Minaret] Followed by a Traverse of Mt. Ritter from the South

FROM MY CAMP at Thousand Island Lake one morning in the latter part of June, I set forth on a ramble southward. Crossing a ridge a few hundred feet in height, I dropped down to Garnet Lake, an extremely beautiful one, oval in form, a mile or more in length, shut in to the north and south by rocky ridges and to the west by the magnificently picturesque form of Mt. Banner rising in sheer walls to an elevation slightly under 13,000 feet above sea level. A brisk wind ruffled its azure water causing it to break energetically against the rocky shores which rise abruptly in massive granite topped by scattered stands of lodgepole pine and mountain hemlock.

After surmounting a second ridge, I began to descend into the valley of Shadow Creek. To the southwest, across the forested canyon, rose the jagged Minarets seeming to issue a challenge as I gazed at them, for they had never been scaled from the eastern side and but once from the western. Below and some distance to the left lay Shadow Lake, a blue expanse of water in a setting of green conifers and gray granite walls.

Upon reaching the floor of the valley, I was surprised at its beauty. A limpid stream of considerable volume plunged in snowy cascades and raced along in scintillating rapids or lingered in deep emerald pools. On either side were groves of tamarack pine with mountain hemlock interspersed in increasing numbers as one advanced up the valley. A second lake— deep, clear and blue—presently came within view, its beauty enhanced by an alpine setting of the jagged Minarets to the southwest and by the dark, massive peaks of Mts. Ritter and Banner to the northwest. Above its sapphire depths stood a grove of very large mountain hemlocks, one of the finest in the Sierra. Entering it I paused for a short time on a bed of red heather which seemed to be more abundant there than almost anywhere in the range. I could not refrain from admiring the rugged beauty of the mature hemlocks and the elegant grace of the young ones, most beautiful of all our alpine conifers.

Continuing on my way, I crossed a stream meandering through grassy meadows and climbed a green slope to the crest

17

of a rocky ridge from which I looked down to the left on Iceberg Lake, of deepest blue, sunk in a bowl-like amphitheatre with a fine grove of mountain hemlocks on one side and a precipitous glacier on the other. From time to time even in midsummer large fragments of ice break away, fall into the lake, and float around in its ultramarine blue water—hence its name.

The ridge became rockier and snow was soon encountered as I pressed on towards the Minarets, which seemed to entice me onward. The highest of them lay directly to the south and rose apparently sheer from a steeply pitching hanging glacier. Presently I came to this glacier and began to trudge up a slope that became steeper as I advanced. The sun was already dropping westward and shadows were falling across the glacier from the jagged pinnacles to the right. Steeply inclined frozen snow soon obliged me to cut steps around a protruding parapet for a distance of several hundred feet. This passed, the gradient became gentler and, being still exposed to sunshine, was sufficiently soft to enable me to progress rapidly.

Upon reaching the upper side of the glacier immediately below the highest Minaret, I spent a short time exploring the bergschrund and then paused for a few minutes to consider my plans. It was already four o'clock. If an attempt were made to climb the peak it might be unsuccessful, but even if it should succeed, the surface of the glacier would be frozen hard upon my return, obliging me to cut my way down, perhaps in darkness, a tedious and somewhat precarious undertaking. Having decided to make the attempt, however, I found a bridge across the bergschrund and with some little difficulty clambered up the rocks directly above it. Thence I worked my way upward along narrow shelves and over steep pitches, sometimes hoisting myself with little more than a finger and a toe hold, and wondering whether I would be able to make the descent so readily. Eventually I reached the crest of the mountain, only to find a deep gash between me and the highest point. As a descent to the gash would be hazardous, I hastened down a ridge paralleling a couloir for about two hundred feet.

In my hurry I almost met with an accident. As I stepped on an apparently firm slab it gave way, but fortunately a firm handhold prevented me from going along with it. It struck my ice axe and rucksack which I had let down over a vertical pitch, and came within an ace of pushing them over the mountainside. This would have been serious, for without an ice axe I would be unable to cross the glacier by night. Eventually finding a ledge leading to the bottom of the couloir, I followed it thither. Although very steep, plenty of handholds enabled me to scale the wall above it with considerable speed and presently I swung up to the crest only a few yards from the summit. It was a rather eerie spot. Only a few feet in diameter, it dropped away sheer for hundreds of feet on every side except the one up which I had climbed.

The sun nearing the horizon cast horizontal rays across the Sierra and from every peak elongated shadows were creeping eastward. To the north a line of sharp spires not much lower than the one on which I was standing extended toward the rugged form of Mt. Ritter, looming sublime against the blue sky. To the left of it stood the picturesque group of Mts. Lyell, Maclure and Roger, their summits lighted up by the evening rays of the sun.

Soon I was on my way down the wall, down the couloir, and along the shelf. By descending somewhat to the east of the route of my ascent, I avoided some of the difficulties encountered on the way up, and in fact few were encountered until I neared the glacier. There I spent a good deal of time finding a way down the steep, smooth rock to the glacier. As I had anticipated, the ice was already frozen hard and darkness was fast settling down over the mountains. I spent about an hour cutting my way across the glacier and around a buttress, but since a thousand feet of steeply inclined snow and ice lay below, it was not advisable to hurry.

The glacier traversed, I picked my way slowly and carefully down a broken cliff, and came at length to a clump of whitebark pines with a nearby lake gleaming through the darkness. As there was plenty of fuel I decided to bivouac for the night although, being on a pass, I would be more or less exposed to the wind. It did blow heavily all night and the temperature was frigid, but the thick growth of trees broke the violence of the wind while a blazing bonfire dispelled the cold. The moon shed a half-radiance on the battlemented Minarets to the west and the dark forms of Ritter and Banner silhoutted against the starry sky to the north.

At daybreak I left my bivouac, passed the lake shining like a mirror in the dawn, and descended a pitch a few hundred feet high. Passing exquisite Iceberg Lake, I swung across the meadows to Lake Ediza. There I ate the remainder of the lunch which I had brought with me from camp on the preceeding day and

19

enjoyed a nap on a sunny bed of heather. Although hungry, I decided to return to camp over the top of Mt. Ritter, 13,156 feet above sea level, by dropping down its northern face and swinging around Mt. Banner to Thousand Island Lake.

After traversing a grove of hemlocks and crossing an alpine meadow down which ran numerous brooks fed by the abundant snow and the glacier above, I clambered up the glaciated benches of a cliff several hundred feet high and trudged across a small glacier to a couloir opening onto it from the north. Up this I turned, making my way at first on snow, then over the rocks which were interesting because of the great variety of igneous rocks among them. Very interesting also were the views of the dark-hued spires of the Minarets immediately below and of the southern Sierra looming vast in the distance. Eventually the couloir widened, opening onto a gradual slope leading up to the summit, which I reached about noon.

The day was extremely pleasant and the view magnificent, extending far down the axis of the range and including most of its major peaks. Near at hand, across the deep gorge of the North Fork of the San Joaquin, the Mt. Lyell group stood sharply outlined against a cerulean sky. To the northeast, past Banner Peak, gleamed the gray-green expanse of Mono Lake in a setting of tawny desert wastes.

After a short pause I dropped down the north face of the peak, then down a broad couloir ending in a steep snow slope, to the saddle between Mt. Ritter and Mt. Banner. Veering to the right, I sped down the snow around the shoulder of Mt. Banner and then picked my way down over the rocks to Thousand Island Lake. Walking across the soft meadow and around the rocky margin of the lake I was fascinated by the alpine beauty of the scene. To my right lay the lake, a scintillating sheet of sapphire dotted with rocky islets. Behind me, crowned with massive white clouds, the steep-walled north face of Mt. Banner was enveloped in afternoon shadows.

A Mountain Ramble Over Mt. Barnard
and Around

Y CAMP WAS IN AN exceptionally beautiful spot at an altitude of slightly over 11,000 feet above the sea in an open stand of intermingled foxtail and lodgepole pines. Up rocky slopes to the east and southeast a scattering of the storm-torn pines, gradually dwindling in size, continued for a few hundred feet and then ceased entirely. Extensive meadows lay on the headwaters of the stream which, teeming with golden trout, flowed past the pines in which I made my camp. Southwestward across the spacious amphitheatre on the headwaters of the Kern, I enjoyed a fine view of the castellated summits of the Kaweahs, the highest of which approach 14,000 feet in elevation.

With no very definite plans in mind for the day, after a breakfast of mountain fare—the *pièce de résistance* were pansized golden trout caught in the nearby brook—I left camp and began to pick my way in a southeasterly direction through foxtail pines and over strips of talus. The angular blocks of granite in this area appeared to be larger than average. Among the rocks, their apparently fragile forms swaying airily in every breath of morning breeze, I came upon numerous clumps of columbine with flowers of delightfully pure tones of white, yellow, and orange.

From a thicket of alpine willow two bucks, a large and a small one, suddenly darted and went bounding away over a shoulder of Mt. Barnard. In summer the deer, especially the bucks, are fond of these high-growing thickets of alpine willow a few feet in height, as they afford both food and shelter.

I ascended the south shoulder of Mt. Barnard. Upon reaching its crest I turned to the left and began to follow the rounded ridge which gradually rises at a very gentle angle to its highest point at its northern end, an altitude of 14,003 feet.

I observed, as I trudged along, an interesting succession of alpine flowers. One after another species ceased, but several continued almost to the top of the mountain. Two of the species encountered, the polemonium and the draba, continue to higher elevations in the Sierra than the summit of Mt. Barnard.

21

Several, however, continued to somewhat higher altitudes than I had previously observed them. At about 12,500 feet I saw an isolated specimen of the jamesia, a shrub with white flowers belonging to the saxifrage family, and another of ocean spray, also a white-flowered shrub, but a spiraea. Both of these were higher than I had seen them elsewhere in the Sierra; higher, in fact, than any other shrub in the range except the wild currant.

For some distance up the gradually ascending ridge I came upon numerous clumps of the exquisite Sierra primrose with flowers splashed with red or violet in the older ones. The hulsea, sometimes called alpine gold, continued up to about 13,800 feet. This is a small member of the sunflower (compositae) family with a maximum height of about a foot, and sunflower-like blossoms an inch in diameter. It is especially interesting because during the summer months it forms the staple diet of the wild sheep, a considerable number of which still range these high-lying crests, in places several thousand feet above the last trees. They devour it, root, stem, and flower, digging out the first with horn or hoof, or both.

At about the same elevation I observed a mat-like growth of the lewisia, with its rosettes of leaves pressed down against the disintegrated granite in which it usually grows, and its small, upturned flowers of pure, waxen white. This was slightly higher than I had remembered seeing it on other Sierra peaks. The alpine penstemon, pride of the Sierra, persisted to about the same elevation. The two most abundant flowers were the polemonium and the hulsea, from 12,500 to 13,500 feet, but the former persisted to within a few feet of the highest point of the mountain.

From some 12,500 feet upward I had observed the footprints, bedding places, and excreta of wild sheep. These were most numerous where the hulsea grew most abundantly. Rather strangely, although it was mid-July, these signs seemed to have held over from the previous year. At these high elevations rain seldom falls, and the melting snow seeps so gently in the disintegrated granite that footprints and other evidence may survive from one year to the next. There was no indication that the sheep had fed upon the hulsea or other alpine plants during this season.

Having reached the top of the mountain, an altitude of 14,003 feet, I sat down on a rock and began to eat luncheon. Mt. Barnard has the reputation of being the easiest of ascent of the 14,000 foot peaks of the Sierra. Its summit, as is the case of

22

all the higher peaks of the Sierra, commands a spacious panorama. I looked along the crest of the Sierra from Mt. Whitney northward to the Palisades and beyond. Northeastward only a short distance the imposing form of Mt. Williamson projected eastward from the crest of the range. Immediately below to the west lay the wide amphitheatre on the headwaters of the Kern, and beyond it the ragged line of high peaks of the Great Western Divide.

Luncheon over, I descended eastward to an alpine basin lying about 500 feet below the summit of Mt. Barnard. There I came upon more evidence of mountain sheep. From the basin I continued southward up an unnamed peak 13,747 feet in elevation, and southward from it to a saddle. All along the crest the polemonium grew abundantly and the hulsea was more plentiful than usual. I saw frequent evidence of wild sheep, but none that I could identify for certain as having been made during the present season. I wondered when the bighorn which usually spend a few summer weeks, perhaps several months, would appear.

From the saddle, I descended a cliff to the southwest. On its ledges also I found abundant evidence of wild sheep. Near the base of the cliff, lying at an altitude of slightly over 11,000 feet, I came upon a deep blue lake, roughly oval in form and perhaps a third of a mile in length. This was Wallace Lake, famous among California fishermen for its large golden trout. On a moist slope a short distance above the lake I saw a corn lily at perhaps the highest elevation that I have ever seen it growing in the Sierra.

From the lower end of the lake I swung northwestward. As the sun sank toward the line of rough-hewn peaks of the Great Western Divide westward across the wide amphitheatre on the headwaters of the Kern, I rounded the south shoulder of Mt. Barnard and continued downward through a scattering of foxtail pines, past several clumps of alpine willow to my camp.

My day's trip had not been at all spectacular as I climbed Mt. Barnard from the southwest and gradually circled around to my point of departure. To a mountaineer Mt. Barnard is a mere bump. The only real climbing that I encountered was on one or two cliffs. It was in fact rather a mountain ramble, and although I travelled a considerable distance, a rather leisurely one. I had concentrated my attention on plant and animal life, and derived considerable enjoyment therefrom.

23

An Ascent of the Black Kaweah

Of THE NUMEROUS picturesque groups of peaks in the Sierra Nevada, probably none is more striking than the Kaweahs, which project eastward toward the Kern River from a point about midway along the Great Western Divide. They are a remnant of a range that preceded the present Sierra Nevada. Several of the higher peaks approach 14,000 feet in elevation. The most spectacularly rugged and the most challenging from a climbing standpoint is the most westerly of the group—the Black Kaweah.

I have climbed all of the group a number of times and have always tried to make an ascent of the Black Kaweah when I happened to pass that way. On one of these occasions I left the Sierra Club camp in the Five Lakes basin a few miles to the south, accompanied by several companions. At first our way led down a steep trail through a scattering of whitebark pine, but soon there appeared the tall spires of red fir with their rich purple-red bark, its still more spire-like cousin, the silver fir, and the wide-branched mountain pine, akin to the sugar pine. Flowers also seemed to be unusually abundant. Along streamlets that gushed from springs and went leaping down rocky slopes, the red-flowered *bryanthus*, the white ledum or Labrador-tea, and the blue lupin grew in profusion. On granite ledges and coign-like niches appeared the magenta flowers of the pride of the Sierra, most beautiful of the mountain penstemons, whose glow impart a touch of vivid color to many a stretch of sober gray granite in the Hudsonian zone.

We followed a zigzag trail to the bottom of the Big Arroyo, crossed the stream and slowly made our way up the opposite slope. As we approached the north rim of the gorge, foxtail pine became abundant. The scattered lines of their rich red boles springing from the rock-strewn terrain and upholding their storm-torn boughs against the background of the rugged mass of the Black Kaweah formed a scene so striking as to be long remembered.

On a rocky point overlooking a stream that tumbled down its channel we made camp, kindling our fire underneath a fox-

24

tail pine and clearing places amid thickly strewn granite boulders to bivouac. As night approached the level rays of the setting sun streamed through the scattered ranks of foxtail pines, causing their reddish boles to glow in still richer hues. Gradually lifting, they gilded the dark summit of the Black Kaweah towering above us some distance to the north. Gray twilight slowly crept over the hushed solitude of the mountains until the moon, appearing above the main crest of the Sierra, flooded with silver light both the Kaweahs and the long serrated line of the Great Western Divide. We retired early and were astir shortly after dawn on the following morning.

Breakfast disposed of as expeditiously as possible, we swung on our rucksacks and began to pick our way over stretches of glaciated rock and morainal debris toward a cirque to our left. Presently we were confronted by a tier of cliffs running at right angles below a large couloir up which our route lay. A ledge runs obliquely up the face of the cliff to the lower end of the coloir, but although I had followed the route previously, I had forgotten the location of the ledge. With a little reconnoitering, however, I succeeded in finding it and we had little difficulty in filing upward along it to the foot of the couloir.

This chute cuts deeply into the face of the Black Kaweah and continues all the way up to its headwall a few hundred feet below the summit. The mountain is composed for the most part of dark metamorphic rock which is somewhat friable. As it contains some magnesium, particularly in the rock joints, the exposed surfaces are smooth and when wet have a sort of soapy slipperiness. The floor of the couloir was pretty well covered with loose rock debris and the angle so steep that a climber was obliged to move cautiously in order to avoid dislodging rocks, which would go ricocheting down the chute, usually starting others, perhaps precipitating a small rock slide and endangering those below. On the last climb I had made of the Black Kaweah we were caught in an almost blinding snowstorm near the summit. We came down the couloir to the accompaniment of cracking thunder, and flashing lightening; presently, water from melting snow began to pour into the couloir, flowing down it, threatening to start a rock slide. Neither hit by lightening, although it struck a pinnacle perilously near us, nor caught in a rock slide in the deep couloir, we emerged safely from the lower end of the chute.

25

After following the floor of the couloir for some distance, we abandoned it and began to scale a precipitous wall to the left. This eventually brought us to a jagged arête that in some places dropped away in a cliff hundreds of feet in depth. We were then a few hundred feet below and within plain view of the summit. When a short distance below it, we cut across to the right to a point only a few feet below the latter. There we encountered an obstacle in the form of a large rock so insecurely poised that a mere touch might send it crashing down the mountainside. After picking my way delicately around it, I gave it a slight shove. Away it went, ricocheting wildly down a steep chute followed by a troop of smaller rocks clattering along in its wake. This was a case of what I sometimes dub "house cleaning." The insecurely poised rock out of the way, the remnants of the party came along without encountering any hazard.

A very short escalade directly upward then brought us to the top of the mountain, a narrow point of ice-shattered rock only a few yards in diameter and 13,751 feet above the sea. It commands a panorama of amazing extent. From Mt. Langley, some fifteen miles to the southeast across the wide amphitheatre on the headwaters of the Kern, the eye follows the main crest of the Sierra northward and past Mt. Whitney, the highest, past Mt. Williamson, the second highest mountain in the Sierra, some fifty miles northward past the Palisades, the most ruggedly spectacular of the higher groups of peaks of the Sierra, onward and slightly westward past other groups of high peaks in the southern portion of the Sierra, eventually coming to rest at the mountains of the Yosemite area, hazy in the distance. It commands an unsurpassed view down it into the spacious circular amphitheatre, sown with numerous lakes, on the headwaters of the Kern and far southward along its course through undulating forest-clad mountains. Westward it looks downward across the gradually declining west slope of the Sierra to the broad hazy valley of the San Joaquin to the long line of the even-crested Coast Range beyond it.

In contrast to our experience on the Black Kaweah when we were caught in a terriffic storm shortly after leaving the summit, on this ascent the weather could scarcely have been more delightful. The sky was cloudless, the sunshine warm, the atmosphere of wonderful clarity. For an hour or more we lingered on the narrow summit, leisurely eating luncheon and surveying the immense panorama of mountain, valley, and desert outspread in

26

a radius of a hundred miles or more in every direction from our lofty vantage point.

We then began to retrace our way down the steep headwall of the couloir, along the narrow knife edge, and thence down to the lower and deeper portion of the almost gorge-like couloir, in the latter picking our way carefully among the loose and often insecurely poised rock debris and sometimes across treacherously smooth and perhaps slippery surfaces. The afternoon sun shone bright into the couloir. As we carefully made our way downward we noticed numerous clusters of the exquisitely beautiful white and pink Sierra primrose in the clefts of the frost-shattered rocks. Now and then we heard the sweetly plaintive calls of the rosy finch, bird par excellence of the high peaks of the Sierra. Seldom does one ascend any of its lofty summits without encountering at least several of them feeding and flitting about on the very summits.

Eventually we debouched from the lower end of the couloir and filed down the narrow ledge to the talus slope at the base of the mountain and thence across several miles of somewhat broken terrain to our camp among the foxtail pines, looking down into the deep, glacier-cut gorge of the Big Arroyo. Our ascent and descent of the Black Kaweah, one of the finest peaks of the Sierra, had been one of unalloyed pleasure.

Up the South Face of Mt. Lyell

At five o'clock in the morning one head after another popped up above the dwarfed and contorted whitebark pine at timberline on the headwaters of Rush Creek in the Sierra Nevada. Most of the preceeding day had been spent by the party of a dozen or so of us crossing some ten miles of mountains, in large part still buried deep in snow although it was the 8th of July.

We had reached timberline late in the afternoon at an elevation of about 11,000 feet and after some reconnoitering had come upon this thicket of *albicaulis* pine on a slope which, due to its southwesterly exposure, was free from snow. As a camping spot it had one special advantage in that the members of our party, at the expense of a little work, were able to make themselves snug sleeping quarters—*boudoirs,* we called them. Underneath the low hanging boughs of the pines we laid our sleeping bags on pine needles upwards of a foot in depth. The one disadvantage of the site was that we were obliged to carry water from the outlet of a frozen lake about a hundred and fifty yards distant.

Mt. Lyell, the highest peak in Yosemite National Park, rose several miles northwest of us. Although usually it had been ascended from the north, we decided to attempt to reach its summit by scaling the precipitous south face in order to avoid going around from the east where we were camped.

Breakfast prepared and eaten, we shouldered our rucksacks and ropes and picked up our ice axes. After crossing the frozen lake, we picked our way up over a tier of cliffs almost entirely free from snow. Beyond these, however, we found another frozen lake which we crossed, to begin our trudge up a steep snow slope. This was followed by another basin and another steep snow-buried slope. These traversed, we found ourselves in a bowl-shaped basin or cirque immediately below the crest of the Sierra. Another long pull of perhaps a thousand feet brought us to it.

We looked southwest across the headwaters of the Merced River far down its course, and to the northwest, less than a mile distant, up to Mt. Lyell. We perched on rocks and surveyed its steep front carefully. Three routes up it seemed feasible but, unable to decide on one among them, we decided to advance to a wide chute which we could either climb or cross to one or another of the several alternative routes.

While picking our way over the intervening rocks and snow, I carefully scanned the face of Mt. Lyell to the right. This appeared to be the most challenging of the three possibilities, and both Jack Riegelhuth, a member of the Rock Climbing Section of the Sierra Club, and myself felt certain that it could be scaled. Therefore, having reached the chute, we soon swung onto the precipitous face above and to the right of it. Pursuing a course running diagonally upward to the crest of a great buttress which extends southward from the top of the mountain, we now made a direct escalade upward from ledge to ledge, then followed along narrow shelves. Fairly difficult at first, the climbing became more so as we rose steadily toward the crest. Occasionally we were obliged to use steeply shelving ledges and now and then to scale vertical pitches provided with none too many hand- and footholds.

When we had gained the crest, a narrow knife edge from which we could look far down a very steep couloir, we halted until Jack should have time to bring up the rear of the line. The top of the mountain was here directly above us, apparently less than 500 feet away. A narrow ledge ran along the couloir below us to within several hundred feet of its upper end, from which it seemed possible to climb over the headwall to the summit of the mountain. Our party safely reached the crest of the buttress, filed along the narrow ledge and, having gained the floor of the couloir, began to scale the precipitous headwall. Since this was well broken into shelves, we passed rapidly upward from one to another until presently we emerged on the crest of another buttress.

From here we traversed into another couloir and upon clambering out over the head of this, suddenly we came within sight of the cairn on top of the mountain, only a few rods above and to the right of us. Within a few minutes the entire party had swarmed out of the couloir and onto the top of Mt. Lyell, an altitude of 13,090 feet above the sea.

As the sunshine fell warm on the granite rock of the narrow top of the mountain we were soon comfortably settled here and there. Well occupied with surveying the magnificent panorama extending far in every direction, we stowed away luncheon with the usual avidity of mountaineers. Immediately below us to the north, extending upward to within 500 feet of the top of the mountain, lay the Mt. Lyell Glacier, second largest in the Sierra Nevada. Across this a few miles in an air-line lay the headwaters of the Tuolumne River. Below, running in a northwesterly direction, were the Tuolumne Meadows, a few miles in length and terminating westward in the upper end of the Grand Canyon of the Tuolumne, a great twenty-mile gorge upwards of a vertical mile in depth, ending in the Hetch Hetchy, once a beautiful valley, now a reservoir. Beyond the Tuolumne lay the rugged mountains of the northern portion of the Park. To the southwest from Lyell we looked across the headwaters of the North and Middle Forks of the San Joaquin River to the lofty peaks, grouped together in a great massif, of the southern Sierra Nevada.

Luncheon finished, we decided to descend, or rather to begin the descent, by dropping down the northeastern shoulder of the mountain to the glacier. This we found to entail several hundred feet of fairly difficult rock climbing, but we soon reached the bergschrund of the glacier, whence we sprang to firm snow from the snow and ice arched over its cavity. Along the steep incline of the upper portion of the glacier we traversed eastward to the head of a couloir which we knew to be east of the divide between the headwaters of the Merced River and those of Rush Creek. However, the upper portion of this was precipitous and appeared to drop off part way down for possibly a hundred feet. We decided, nevertheless, to descend it.

We went down over alternating pitches of rock and steeply inclining snow into which we were obliged to cut steps, for several hundred feet to the brink of the anticipated drop-off which proved to be some fifty feet in height. After running a sling rope—several wrappings of quarter-inch manila rope—around a boulder at the brink of the drop, we threaded one of our 100 foot alpine ropes through the sling and threw the rope doubled down over the step-like drop. I slid down the doubled rope while Jack remained above to supervise the "mountaineers' escalator" from above.

Meanwhile, below them I was busy cutting steps down the precipitous snow incline. Within several hundred feet, however, the angle of the snow decreased sufficiently to enable me to glissade with safety. I therefore went shooting down it, checking myself every hundred feet or thereabouts either by the orthodox method of using my ice axe or by availing myself of the Christiania turn of the skier.

When about two-thirds of the way down the chute, I halted to see how the party was faring. Down they came, some slowly and deliberately, picking their way, others attempting to glissade as I had done. Several of them, not being masters of the technique of glissading or lacking the suitable equipment, appeared to be losing control and in imminent danger of colliding against one or the other wall of the chute. Fortunately, however, none suffered worse than a head-over-heels tumble. This put a stop to their glissading for some distance, but when the angle became somewhat less steep, all went shooting merrily down the remainder of the chute and out onto the basin below.

Alternately crossing basins and glissading down the step-like intervening slopes, we descended rapidly toward camp in the warm afternoon sunshine. Soon we reached the first frozen lake and before long had arrived at the head of the one immediately below our camp. Partly across but partly around it—it was beginning to break up in places—we strode along to our camp in the thicket of whitebark pine. Our day had indeed been a varied one, with the crossing and recrossing of miles of snow in July, and the scaling of the precipitous south face of Mt. Lyell by a route hitherto untrodden by the foot of man.

Southward Over the Kings-Kern Divide and Up Mt. Stanford

Aᴛᴇʀ ᴀ ᴛᴏɪʟsᴏᴍᴇ ᴄʟɪᴍʙ on the 10th of July up the rough abandoned trail over Harrison Pass at an elevation of 12,000 feet above the sea, I set down my heavy pack and looked about for a mountain to climb. A short distance to the east Mt. Stanford with its twin peaks extends northward from the Kings-Kern Divide into the great amphitheatre on the headwaters of Bubbs Creek. As this would afford an excellent and not-too-long climb and would offer unusually fine views from both summits, I was not long in deciding to ascend it.

As I trudged eastward along the crest of the divide over disintegrated granite with numerous frost-riven rocks scattered upon it, I was impressed by the unusual abundance of the polemonium. Springing upward from the granite sand among the shattered rocks, its rounded clusters of vivid blue flowers with their spicy fragrance were everywhere conspicuous. A touch of yellow was added by a compositae, a dimunitive sunflower, and by the hulsea whose sturdy small form contrasted with the elegant beauty of its single flower.

An easy ascent of about a hundred and fifty feet brought me to the summit of Mt. Stanford's twin peaks. A narrow point, it drops away sheer to the east and west, but has a narrow broken arête running northward to what appears to be a slightly higher peak. The summit attained, I paused for a few minutes to survey the great mountain panorama. Northward it extended to the mountains of the Yosemite upwards of a hundred miles distant; southward along the highest portion of the crest of the Sierra past Mt. Whitney and far beyond undulating forested mountains on the middle portion of the Kern.

Leaving the summit, I continued northward along the crest of the jagged arête. Deep gashes, however, caused me to abandon it in favor of an almost horizontal ledge running along the sheer eastern face. This was easily negotiated, but required some caution as it was strewn with loose rock which required little encouragement to go crashing over the precipice below, in all probability taking the incautious mountaineer along.

At the farther end of the ledge, a short escalade brought me to the summit of the more northerly peak. A narrow point

32

also, it had a jagged arête running northward for several miles and eventually terminating in the East Vidette. Here also among the frost-shattered rocks I found the polemonium growing in unusual abundance, clinging to every nook and cranny where there was a suggestion of soil. Except for the distant sound of falling water, deep silence pervaded the mountains. Now and then, however, I heard the cheerful notes of the rosy finch or the merry chatter of the rock wren, both of which are in the habit of ascending to the highest summits of the Sierra.

For an hour or more I remained on the summit eating luncheon, basking in the warm sunshine, and enjoying the vast panorama of mountain and valley extending in every direction. Soft white clouds, suffused with bright sunshine, floated lazily through a deep blue sky. As I wished to make camp somewhere in the amphitheatre on the headwaters of the Kern, it was necessary for me to cut short my sojourn on the top of the mountain.

Clambering down over the broken rocks to the south of the summit, I regained the ledge and retraced my way along it to the more southerly peak, and from it returned westward along the crest of the divide to my pack which I had left on Harrison Pass. Southward I continued from the latter into the great basin on the headwaters of the Kern.

Soon I reached South American Lake lying at an altitude of 12,000 feet above the sea. Although it was the 10th of July this was still entirely covered with ice. Much of the way down from the pass, in fact, I had come over snow. Continuing southward from the lake, I soon reached its lower margin and after traversing some rough rocks, eventually came to meadows where grass was just beginning to spring up.

After skirting several lakes, I came to a small one picturesquely ensconced in a rocky setting of glaciated granite upon which stood scattered clumps of dwarfed, wind-torn *albicaulis* pines. This would be an excellent spot for a high mountain camp —perhaps I should rather say bivouac—and it was unnecessary for me to go farther.

I looked northward across the shimmering surface of the lakelet and up the slopes gradually ascending to the Kings-Kern Divide, running east and west, while sunset light glowed on the couloir-fluted face of Mt. Ericsson on the crest. A pink glow overspread the loftier summit of Mt. Stanford, lingered for a while, and then gradually faded into sober gray, as the shadows of night crept over the craggy mountains.

33

Up the Rugged Canyon of George Creek

O<small>N THE SECOND OF JULY</small> a friend, Homer Erwin, and I drove westward up the gradually rising piedmont slope. The sand road which we were following terminated on its upper margin near where George Creek debouches from a narrow granite-walled gorge at the lower end of a canyon with the same name. Here, at an elevation of some 6,500 feet above the sea, the east front of the southern and loftiest portion of the Sierra extends from Mt. Williamson on the north, southward past Mt. Whitney—a distance of about a dozen miles—and onward in the same direction to Mt. Langley, the most southerly of the 14,000 foot peaks of the Sierra.

To our right, as we stood on the margin of the stream, the southeastern shoulder of Mt. Williamson swept up to its summit, an elevation of 14,375 feet, a continuous rise of some 8,000 feet. Abreast of Mt. Whitney only a few miles to the south a precipitous fault scarp has been weathered westward a few miles, in consequence of which Mt. Whitney stands withdrawn to the head of the canyon of Lone Pine Creek. Mt. Williamson, on the other hand, thrusts eastward from the crest of the Sierra for some distance and then drops directly to the western margin of Owens Valley. As viewed from the latter, therefore, Mt. Williamson is the most spectacular of the higher peaks on the crest of the Sierra.

We planned to ascend the rugged trailless canyon of George Creek to its headwaters and from a camp established there explore and climb the surrounding mountains. As in the case of a number of canyons along the southern Sierra Nevada, the glacier that came down it did not have sufficient volume and momentum to plow the lower portion of the canyon into a pronounced U-shaped cross section. The narrow gorge from which George Creek came tumbling out no doubt has been cut by the stream since glacial days. Because the creek filled the floor of the little gorge, we could not readily ascend it. The glacier also had failed to remove a ridge coming down from Mt. Williamson to the right. To ascend the canyon it was therefore necessary to cross this ridge and descend its farther side to the floor of the canyon above it, involving a climb of perhaps a thousand feet up a loose and rather steep slope of disintegrated granite.

Swinging on our rather heavy knapsacks we began to work upward through a scattered growth of piñon pine and mountain mahogany. Both on account of the loose footing and the hot sunshine which fell on our backs and was reflected upward from the slope into our faces, our rate of speed was not at all phenomenal.

The rounded crest of the ridge gained, we looked down into the narrow floor of the canyon beyond. The stream that came bounding sonorously down under a canopy of birch and willow pretty well filled the latter. Rather than to force our way up it, it seemed better to us to contour along the north-facing slope. This we immediately proceeded to do. The going was slow, however, since the disintegrated granite tended to slide downward beneath our weight.

We made our way upward, gradually approaching the floor of the canyon. The latter widened, and as evening approached at an elevation of perhaps 9,500 feet we reached the mouth of a stream coming in from the south. Immediately above its outlet lay a little flat upon which stood a grove of silver fir. As this was sufficiently high for a base camp and the grove with the brook cascading past it would form an excellent camping place, it was unnecessary to go farther.

It was, in fact, not only an excellent but a fascinating camping spot. To the north the canyon wall rose steeply for perhaps 2,000 feet and its crest was surmounted by a long line of serrated granite spires. To the south rose great granite crags. To the east we looked down the deep canyon and across the wide floor of Owens Valley to the Inyo Mountains, immediately beyond the latter. The atmosphere was one of profound seclusion. Although we were only a few miles from a highway, we had a feeling of being remote from all evidences of civilization. As the sun set the long line of sharp pinnacles, already pink from a trace of hematite in their feldspar, glowed roseate in the rays of the declining sun far above the shadow-filled depths of the canyon.

Early on the following morning we were on our way up the floor of the canyon. This had widened considerably and became broken into the step and tread formation usual in glaciated high mountain canyons. Gently declining inclinations were separated by steep drops of several hundred feet or more, down which a glacier had once come tumbling in spectacular ice falls. The floors of the treads were green with upspringing grass and clumps of alpine willow just then bursting into leaf. The meadows were dotted with the vivid green leaves and the nodding lavender flowers of the shooting star. Here and there mats of *bryanthus* were becoming masses of bright red, spicily-scented clusters of flowers. From both sides of the canyon numerous streams cascaded sonorously down precipitous slopes.

Upon reaching timberline, we veered to the right in order to gain the crest of a ridge which we knew led directly up to the summit of Mt. Williamson. At an elevation of some 12,000 feet we came upon numerous clumps of the vivid blue flowers of the polemonium, alpine flower par excellence of the Sierra Nevada. Beginning at an altitude of some 12,000 feet it continues upward on the highest peaks in one place at least to 14,200, the only flower in the Sierra except the draba which succeeds in doing so. Scattered about on the granite sand were numerous hulsea, sometimes called alpine gold.

After following the even-crested ridge for some distance we swung to the right to avoid a cliff. The latter flanked, we continued upward over a moderately steep slope covered with broken granitic rocks, and sooner than we expected, found ourselves standing on the summit of Mt. Williamson. The ascent from camp had been a long one—upwards of 5,000 vertical feet —but we had encountered no technical difficulties. The climb had been for the most part an inordinately long trudge up steep slopes.

The view obtained from the top of Mt. Williamson is one of the finest in the Sierra Nevada. Projecting as it does eastward from the main crest of the Sierra, it affords un unsurpassed prospect of the great, gorge-furrowed escarpment of the southern Sierra, the loftiest portion of the range. The eye follows more than a hundred miles of its jagged crest extending from Mt. Langley northward and slightly westward to the mountains of the Yosemite area. Eastward and southeastward one overlooks a vast area of alternating desert mountains and intervening basins. Westward the view extends down the forest-clad slope of the Sierra across the San Joaquin Valley to the long, even line of the Coast Range; southward and southwestward across the amphitheatre on the headwaters of the Kern and far down the latter flanked on either side by undulating conifer-clad mountains. The day of our ascent was exquisitely beautiful. The sky

36

was cloudless and a deep blue; the summit, except for an occasional gust of rather cool wind, was pleasantly warm, but we did not linger long upon it as we wished to scale the two easterly and somewhat lower peaks of Mt. Williamson.

We hastened down a rather moderate slope to the base of the first peak. A somewhat interesting escalade quickly brought us to the narrow summit scaled but once previously. Between it and the other peak a gash, perhaps a hundred and fifty feet deep, intervened. As the precipitous face of the opposite peak looked rather forbidding, we scanned it carefully with a pair of binoculars in search of a feasible route up it and after selecting one, we descended to the intervening notch. Reaching an impasse, however, we returned to the notch by letting ourselves down from ledge to ledge. Crossing a narrow basin about midway along the face, we threaded our way upward without encountering anything special in the way of difficulty.

This peak proved to be a narrow point breaking away on three sides in sheer cliffs. From it we obtained impressive views down into the deep canyon of Shepherd Creek Canyon and into that of George Creek from which we had come. Immediately below lay a moderately steeply inclining declivity flanked by sheer crags. It was a remnant of an ancient landscape raised to its present position by the uplift of the Sierra. It was of special interest to me since the floor of the valley 10,000 feet below looked upward to see the rays of the setting sun streaming across the crest of the Sierra and gilding the rocky facets in roseate hues. For many thousands of years it had glowed thus at sunrise and sunset, but we were the first men to witness the scene.

The sun had already swung well to the west and we did not remain long on the summit. Swinging on our rucksacks and rope, we retraced our way down the face of the peak, clambered down a precipitous drop from which we ascended to the crest of the long ridge we had come up early in the day and followed it down to the headwaters of George Creek. While descending a grassy slope we came upon a grouse with a brood of very young fledglings. As we approached, they squatted down in the short grass, but we could easily pick them up. They were so young and unsophisticated that they showed no symptoms of alarm.

In early evening we reached our pleasant camp in the grove of silver fir overlooking the cascading stream. Perched as it was in a deep canyon, far up on the rugged eastern escarpment of the Sierra, it had an atmosphere of remote aloofness that was fascinating.

Next morning we were again on our way up the canyon and into the cirques on its headwaters. After passing along a ridge we ascended through a stretch of limber pines, rather common at moderately high elevations on ridges running eastward from the crest of the Sierra. Traversing an expanse of green meadow and pushing our way through several thickets of alpine willow, we reached timberline. We still came upon patches of green where streams gushed from the ground or flowed from underneath melting masses of snow. Dotting the grass were nodding lavender-blossomed cyclamens and sometimes clumps of vivid yellow-flowered mimulus. Higher up we entered what appeared to be a vegetationless basin, but there we came upon great numbers of delicately beautiful polemonium and numerous small but stalwart-looking hulsea.

After crossing a basin, we clambered over a belt of frost-riven rocks to the summit of Mt. Barnard, 14,003 feet in elevation. Although this is not a commanding peak—a bump mountaineers would call it—it affords a wide view, well worth its ascent. It is usually, however, climbed from the west or southwest up easy ridges. Imprinted on loose disintegrated granite we observed numerous tracks of mountain sheep. During the summer months a considerable number of these occur along the main crest of the Sierra from Mt. Whitney to Mt. Russell, the first peak north of Mt. Whitney. For some reason or other, on some fifty ascents of the latter made from every direction, I have never seen a trace of bighorn there. These dozen miles or so of the high crest consist in large measure of fragments of summit-plateau—so geologists term them—usually covered with a layer of disintegrated granite, from which spring a sparse growth of small alpine plants, which continue in considerable numbers up to an altitude of 13,500 feet and in the case of the polemonium and draba to 14,200 feet. I once saw the footprints of a wild sheep within a few feet of the top of Mt. Russell, an elevation of 14,190 feet. The only vegetation surviving were several flowering polemonium plants. Perhaps the wild sheep, like featherless biped mountaineers, had ascended the peak to enjoy the view.

After surveying the fine view from the top of Mt. Barnard we descended northeastward to a basin and from it climbed a nameless peak, 13,983 feet in height. It commands an excellent view of the sheer east face—the only impressive one—of Mt. Tyndall, 14,025 feet in altitude, and another of the couloir-fluted western face of Mt. Williamson to the northeast, apparently little more than a stone's throw distant.

After a short tarry, we left the summit and soon were enjoying long glissades down over slopes of snow. These were followed by others covered with granite sand down which we trudged in rather prosaic fashion. Soon, however, we reached the realm of grass and a little later that of trees. As we neared camp a doe and a fawn glided silently through a small stand of limber pine. Early in the morning a large buck came within an ace of stepping over the drab-colored sleeping bag of my friend but suddenly identifying its human occupant, appeared to be more startled than he.

Upon arriving at camp we got together our packs and were soon making—perhaps I should rather say breaking—our way down the canyon. For the sake of change we had decided to descend the south side of the canyon. On occasional short halts in struggling through thick brush that clothed the mountainside, we noted the bright scarlet hue of penstemon, wild fuchsia, and gilia. To our left, some distance below, the stream, brimful from the melting snows, cascaded sonorously down under its overarching canopy of birches. Eventually we crossed the north side of the stream and after climbing the protruding ridge descended from it to the upper margin of the piedmont slope.

We had been gone only three days, but these were days full of pleasant exploring and climbing worth travelling far to enjoy.

The First Ascent of Thunderbolt Peak, The North Palisade

From our camp among the Big Pine Lakes at an elevation of some 11,000 feet above sea level, across an alpine amphitheatre several miles distant, towered the great spires of the North Palisade. Of the three major ones, the highest attains an elevation of 14,242 feet, the second over 14,000 feet and the third somewhat less. Since the first ascent in 1903 by Joseph LeConte, Jr. and his party, the first has been ascended several dozen times from the south and a few times from the north, the second but twice from any direction, while the rounded monolith forming the summit of the third had never been climbed. Early one morning toward the end of August, 1931, nine of us filed out from camp, intent upon scaling this third, the most westerly, peak of the North Palisade.

The sharp mountain tops which but a short time earlier were flushed with the light of dawn, stood clearly silhouetted against a light blue sky. This, however, was no guarantee that the weather would continue fair throughout the day. In fact, in view of the storms which had been sweeping over the Sierra for upwards of a week, we were not any too hopeful that it would do so.

After swinging around the rocky hillock upon which our camp was situated, we passed through a strip of lodgepole and whitebark pines around a meadow, and began to hike southward up a trail leading towards the glacier at the base of the North Palisade. The trail switchbacked up a rocky slope to a hanging valley, followed it for several hundred yards, then zigzagged eastward up to the crest of a rounded ridge along which it continued southward to within half a mile of the glacier. From the terminus of the trail we picked our way over an area of glaciated granite and a stretch of loose moraine to the margin of the glacier which was almost devoid of snow and seamed with numerous streams running down tortuous channels cut into it. Throughout its upper half it was rent by a large number of open crevasses but none of these were of any great width, except the bergschrund along the base of the cliffs.

A few white clouds rose above the tops of the mountains

as we scanned the walls to the east of the peak which we wished to scale. Eventually we decided to attempt to reach a large notch immediately east of it by making our way up the right wall of the couloir leading to the notch or, alternatively, along the crest of the rib above the wall.

The bergschrund having been filled by a rock slide at the point where we decided to cross, we readily traversed it and, by swinging somewhat to the left, reached the mouth of the chute. Its floor could be climbed easily but in order to avoid rocks which might come ricocheting down it, we preferred to pick our way along the wall. This we found interesting but not especially difficult climbing. Having "roped up" into three parties, we steadily made our way upward. Two of the ropes scaled the wall and followed the crest while the third, there now appearing to be little danger of rocks falling in the chute, continued up the latter for some distance and then scaled the rather precipitous wall at its head, emerging in the great notch, our first objective.

To the east of us the second highest peak towered in a great spire while to the west, the one which we contemplated climbing rose in a great granite blade apparently almost sheer. By this time, however, the sky had become overcast and masses of dark, threatening clouds were approaching from the southwest. We therefore lost little time in beginning our attack upon the peak. The first few hundred feet were much less precipitous than they had appeared from below, and the rock surface was broken by so many grooves and crevices that we scaled it with comparative ease. At the upper end of this steep pitch, we were obliged either to swing around a buttress on an exposed face with few rounded holds, or to traverse to a couloir some fifty yards to the left and ascend that. Two of the ropes swung around the buttress, the third availed itself of the traverse and the couloir. Several hundred feet of scrambling over great rocks then brought both parties to the jagged summit arête and an additional few hundred feet along this, to the foot of the rounded monolith which forms the top of the peak. But the storm was almost upon us.

Arriving at the base of the monolith, one member of the party leaned across a deep crevice at its base and braced himself against the rock, forming a *courte echelle*, enabling several in turn to mount upon his shoulders and then scramble, or rather crawl, depending almost entirely upon friction, to the summit. Static electricity presently began to hum and thunder began to crash. We beat a hasty retreat eastward along the crest in search of shelter. As we hurried along, a thunderbolt flashed past in disconcerting, if not dangerous, proximity to one of the members of the party. A heavy wind drove thickly flying snowflakes into our faces.

Finding a point from which we could easily descend for some distance on the south face, we did so, presently coming upon a ledge with an overhang above it. As this was enough to protect us from any thunderbolt which might strike the summit and afford some shelter from the storm, we crowded together beneath it, a rather bedraggled-looking group. Within half an hour, the storm ceased for a time and we returned to the top of the mountain. The summit monolith was now too slippery to permit rubber soles to grip its rounded surface, and the other climbers were reluctantly obliged to forego its ascent.

For the sake of variation, we decided to drop down the west face of the spire, traverse the head of a couloir on the south face of the mountain, and cross a gap to the head of a wide chute on its northern face which, earlier in the season, could be easily descended. Presently the storm was upon us again. The wind blew violently and the snow flew so thickly as to be almost blinding. An ice axe accidentally dislodged went hurtling down over the cliffs. With some difficulty we kept to our plan and reached the head of the chute on the northern wall. The descent went well at first as it was rather easy to go down the rocks on the left and eventually on the right side of the couloir, but as we approached the glacier it seemed necessary to cut steps down a steeply-pitching gradient to the bergschrund which must be crossed in order to reach the glacier proper. In normal weather conditions this would have required only about twenty minutes.

As I began to cut steps with the retrieved ice axe—now broken in half—a rock came ricocheting down the ice and was presently followed by another. The storm had loosened the rocks higher up on the mountain. It being obviously very hazardous to attempt to go down the chute, more especially so because the fog which now overhung the mountains concealed the flying rocks until they were almost abreast of us, we decided to try to find a way down the end of the rock promontory which we had been following. There would, however, be two difficulties to overcome: one, to get down to the foot of the promontory; the other, to get across the bergschrund below it. The former would probably be sheer for some distance and the latter might be so

42

wide and deep as to be a serious, perhaps insurmountable, obstacle.

We walked along the crest of the promontory until we came to a protuberance to which a loop of rope might be attached, so that we could rope down a distance of about fifty feet to the ice, at a point below a projecting buttress which would protect us from rocks coming down the chute. An alpine rope having been threaded through the loop and a safety rope adjusted about his waist, Mr. Underhill, a well-known mountain climber from Harvard University, roped down to the ice. I followed, and Underhill belayed me as I cut steps downward along the margin of the chute. As I neared the end of the rope I came to a rock which would be a good stance (standing place). Down to this a third member of the party came to belay me while I continued to cut steps.

Eventually, I reached a rock above the ice wall which drops into the bergschrund, over which a rope might safely be looped. Using the rope attached to my waist together with another one which was passed down the line, I threw the doubled rope over the rock and let it down into the crevasse, whose bottom I could not see since the ice shelved for some distance before reaching the vertical or overhanging drop. I tossed rocks into the bergschrund which seemed to strike bottom within a reasonable time. The doubled rope was somewhat over fifty feet in length.

With the rope properly adjusted, I took off, going down the upper steeply-shelving portion gradually so as to be able to cut a few steps to assist those following if I should safely get down into the crevasse, or myself, should I be obliged to come back. After going down about thirty feet, I came to the brink of the vertical ice wall. Fortunately, the bottom, apparently firm, was about twenty feet below. I therefore swung over the brink and glided down the rope to the bottom, which did prove to be firm. Luckily, too, the lower lip of the crevasse was at this point only six or eight feet high. The floor was formed of material that had fallen into the crevasse. Only a few rods to one side, however, it dropped away indefinitely.

A way having been prepared, the rest of the party came down the rope in rapid succession. All real danger past, it was rather amusing to watch one after another as they came over the top of the wall and shot down into the crevasse. After climbing out of the crevasse, we gathered up and coiled about three hundred feet of rope and then sped down over the glacier. The clouds were rapidly breaking away, but meanwhile the sun had set. We traversed the glacier as quickly as possible. Beyond it we were overtaken by darkness but with the aid of flashlights made our way to the trail, down which we strode to the valley. The clouds by this time had vanished and the sky shone with myriads of stars glowing brilliantly as they do in alpine regions. We reached camp, somewhat weary perhaps, but not a little elated over the adventures we had experienced and particularly the difficulties surmounted in an unusually thrilling climb. We had ascended a previously unclimbed summit of the North Palisade to which the name Thunderbolt Peak was later given.

Up and Down the North Palisade

OUR SLEEPING BAGS were white with snow as we awakened at daybreak in our bivouac camp along the margin of a lake at an elevation of about 11,500 feet. Soon we were astir building a fire with the wood which we had packed up to camp several hundred feet above the last trees. Morning shafts of light gilded the lofty spires of the North Palisade towering to elevations of more than 14,000 feet a short distance to the south of us across the North Palisade Glacier. The traverse of several of these was our objective for the day.

By seven we were on our way, at first across a meadow which wound in and out among the glaciated rock, thence over a broad strip of moraine and finally across a half mile of glacier to the lower end of a large couloir extending up the precipitous face of the North Palisade to a large, U-shaped notch on its lofty crest. After cutting our way across a large bergschrund we began to make our way up the steeply pitching snow on the floor of a couloir, and becoming somewhat weary of this, picked our way for some distance along ledges on the precipitous wall to the right of the chute. Finally we went up over a steep tongue of rock to the U-shaped notch on the crest of the mountain.

After descending about a hundred feet in the head of a chute on the opposite side of the mountain, we scaled fifty feet of wall to a horizontal ledge. This we followed westward for a few rods and then swung around a buttress to the lower margin of a well-broken face some 500 feet in height. We swung back and forth up this, encountering interesting but not excessively difficult climbing. At its upper margin we emerged on the crest of the mountain about a quarter of a mile southeast of the summit. The crest was narrow and broken by numerous pinnacles. We hastened along it sometimes over the pinnacles, more frequently, however, along ledges skirting their bases, soon reaching the actual foot of the summit of the mountain. The highest point still lay about 250 feet above us. Over, around, and sometimes under huge blocks of granite we continued to within about thirty feet of the top of the mountain where we

45

swarmed up an almost vertical pitch provided with sufficient good holds to render it a comparatively easy escalade from which we walked upward to the narrow point of rock 14,242 feet above the sea.

To the south the mountain dropped away precipitously in a couloir-fluted face for more than fifteen hundred feet to a lake-dotted basin; to the north an even steeper face for an equal distance dropped to the North Palisade Glacier. To the north-west the crest of the mountain continued for upwards of two miles, extremely narrow and cut into numerous spires, several of which attain elevations of more than 14,000 feet. As we wished to scale several more of these, our pause on the highest summit of the mountain was brief.

Picking our way downward along ledges and over huge, masonry-like blocks of granite we soon reached a notch—a deep and rather wide crevice. A long step, however, left this behind us. Continuing obliquely upward we presently reached another notch, beyond which rose the second highest spire of the North Palisade. We forced our way up a rather narrow couloir and reached the base of the summit monolith, which, although broad at its base, tapered gradually to its summit, a two-by-three foot platform thirty feet above us. Even though the monolith appeared difficult to scale from our present perspective, one can easily walk upward over the rough granite surface on the south side to a point where he can actually reach the top. According to mountain ethics, however, except in the case of a dangerous snow cornice or the like, to claim the ascent of a mountain one should sit on, stand on, or at least lie across, the highest point.

The bulge on this monolith is rather disconcerting, especi-ally to climbers who happen to be carrying an excessive amount of avoirdupois. By dint of considerable pawing with hands and feet, I succeeded in pulling myself up to the top from which I could leisurely survey a magnificent panorama. From Mt. Whitney on the south to the Yosemite mountains on the north, from the Coast Range in the west to far out over a succession of desert mountains in the east—I scanned all this from a space measuring three by two feet about 14,242 feet above the sea from which it looks as if you could reach the North Palisade Glacier 1,500 feet below in a single bound. If the climber has taken up a rope attached to his waist, after satiating himself with the view of the magnificent panorama, he can loop the rope around the summit of the monolith and easily rappel down over its sheer face to the base. My two companions, Jules Eichorn and Hans "Dutch" Leschke, were waiting at the base of the monolith. When I reached the base, both climbed it in turn, not only climbed it, but actually stood upright on its narrow summit.

Since we had in view the ascent of two or three more lofty spires, we were soon on our way again, down the west side of the second highest peak. The traverse of the third spire was by no means an easy one. Hastening down the precipitous west face, we continued until we came to the brink of a formidable drop-off. After a bit of reconnoitering, however, we found a ledge running to the left along the steep face of the mountain. This proved to be a good one, except at one point there was a rather disconcerting break a trifle too wide to leap across. As is sometimes the case, it was not so bad as it looked, for we were able to find several hidden handholds by which to swing across a strip of air reaching to the bottom of the mountain. Soon we reached the head of a steep chimney and slithered down it; after some maneuvering we reached the bottom of a deep col.

Beyond this we saw several alternative routes. We decided upon a ledge which was good, except that it vanished into thin air as it rounded the end of a buttress. Availing ourselves of a single handhold, we swung around the end of the buttress over the airspace to terra firma beyond it. Past the buttress we followed other ledges to the foot of a chimney. For a change, this afforded excellent and not-too-difficult climbing. Emerging from its upper end we clambered over a few steep rocks to the crest of the mountain. A narrow traverse brought us to the foot of the third spire. Up this we clambered to its previously untrodden summit. There our stay was brief, for a dark cloud which sometime previously had appeared in the southwest, had begun to assume ominous proportions.

Soon we gained the foot of the monolith of the summit of Thunderbolt Peak. Although not so high, this is even more difficult than the second highest spire on the crest because it is almost sheer and slightly overhanging above its base. We had intended to scale this spire but now a great mass of dark cloud was rapidly approaching. On a previous occasion when the first ascent of the monolith had been made, the weather conditions were somewhat similar. After several members had scaled the rock, while Jules Eichorn was standing near its base, a thunderbolt struck the summit of the mountain. Jules was rather severely shaken but not actually injured. Scrutinizing the face of the rock, we observed a vertical crevice below which a white line zigzagged downward. The disintegrated whiteish material showed that recently another thunderbolt had scored a bull's-eye. Jules, therefore, was not at all eager to repeat his former experience, or possibly be incinerated on top of the monolith. Because of the thunderbolt experience, this mountain has appropriately been called Thunderbolt Peak.

Our hurried route down the north face of the mountain followed a devious course, now down a steep couloir, then a traverse along a steep face, thence down over a precipitous dropoff, then down a couloir for some distance. Fortunately on this occasion we were not overtaken by the storm, as had been the case on the first ascent. The descent ended by a rapid glissade down the wide floor of a steep but open couloir and by a wild leap over the bergschrund running along the upper margin of the North Palisade Glacier.

Across the glacier we filed along and thence to camp, having completed a day replete with an unusual number of thrills. There had been no really close calls, but we had followed a route in large part previously untrodden, and we also had scaled at least one previously unscaled spire.

"Climbing the North Palisade. Huber and Clyde going up the snow chute. 1920." (Francis Farquhar)

"On top of the Milk Bottle, forty-foot Monolith on top of the second-highest peak of the North Palisade." (Clyde negative, taken by Eichorn, August 1931)

Bishop Pass, ca. 1931. (Clyde negative)

"High Trip 1930." (Cedric Wright; courtesy Sierra Club)

"Clyde Peak" *(Peak 13,659) left center, and Middle Palisade, left.* (Norman Clyde)

North Palisade, center. (Norman Clyde)

Clyde Minaret far left, from Lake Ediza. (Norman Clyde)

Summit of Tower Peak, July 1941. (Parker Severson)

When I first got acquainted with Norman I thought it would be a marvelous opportunity to get all the inside dope on mountains of the Sierra Nevada, the Colorado and Wyoming Rockies, the Lewis and the Livingston Ranges, the Bear Tooths of Montana, the Selkirk, Monashee, Caribou, Purcell—just to roll those delicious names of far-off British Columbia ranges around, and now, just across the old cabin from me, was a man who had wandered through those romantic places making solo first ascents! What a gold mine of information . . . Not so. Not really. It's kind of like pulling teeth. One gets a little blood and after a long effort maybe a bit of broken tooth, but the aching arm is scarcely worth it.

Probably what bothered me more than anything about my early basking in the limelight of a hero (I was never able to call him Norm, and few people do. Just last week someone addressed him so, and it seemed strange to me to hear it. Although he has come to my house bi-monthly for two decades and is almost one of the family, he has always carried a little too much awe and a tiny bit of dignified aloofness. One does not carelessly nickname him, and besides, he's somewhat older than I) whose name was a household word in Governmnt Camp, Oregon, at least among a handful of mountain bums of the nineteen thirties, was the fact that Norman seemed too unconcerned with any heroics on his part. Oregon boys are much oriented toward the northern mountains and it was the ambition of all my school chums of any status to climb Robson, but Norman was so matter of fact about it all. He talked of his climbing companions and maybe the hotcakes—no hair-raising escapades at all. One day I pinned him down to naming a peak in the Sierra, selected from the short list I had climbed, to compare with noble Geikie in the Rampart Range of Canada. "Oh it's just about as hard as Mt. McAdie or a little more so, and about twenty times longer."

Not much for a non-mathematically minded man to go on, yet eventually one day there he was in the flesh and blood, climbing just above me. I heard him mutter and thought to myself, "I must move up close to him, for we are on a steep wall and no doubt coming to a tough place, and I must listen for wisdom from the master." We were not roped and with some effort I drew up near him. He was muttering "Ah, the damned old bitch." Excuse my French, but how terribly prosaic and matter of fact. I thought surely he would be commenting on the dizzy space between us and the glacier below, but no . . .

57

Yes, it was often a woman. Somehow he was always in-volved with them, in relation of landlady and tenant, guide and client. These two categories, of course, refer to some years of long and not always smooth negotiations between the various people who ran certain mountain lodges at which Norman was the snowshoveler and watchman during the long, isolated win-ters, and to his numerous trips to the Rockies with a couple of women whom he never seemed able to teach to climb with any-thing near his lowest level of tolerance. More than these were only infrequent and quite casual contacts, but how he could fume at women who presumed to tell a bachelor how to raise petunias. Damned old busybodies!

I'm coming awfully close to saying Norman is cantank-erous, and now that I think of it a second or two, that is just about the best word in the dictionary for him. As far as I know, he has always accepted me and approved of my mountain habits, a very important qualification from his point of view, and he has never uttered a word of criticism against Jules [Eichorn] and certain others of the Sierra Club, with whom he has been on many trips, but the rest, meaning practically the whole rest of the world . . . !

Gary [Leech] and I were surprised to find on first acquain-tance with Norman that he liked to fish. In our single-minded preoccupation with cliffs and glaciers we could not conceive of a true outdoorsman wasting his time on such a pedestrian pur-suit. However, what we did not fully realize was the fact that Norman lived his whole life in the mountains. And the moun-tains are as broad as life, and just as life is much more than a craze for cars or booze, so mountains are more than a speed record for ascending a volcano or a list of 5.9 pitches con-quered. Norman spent all his time in the mountains and was deep into fishing as much as any other aspect of life in the wild. He considered himself a fine fisherman, and indeed he was. He would not fish unless they were biting. He would lie all after-noon in the sun reading Dumas in French, gazing out across the lake to check for ripples, and when he thought there was enough breeze on the surface for fly fishing he would be off for one circuit of the lake and return with his limit of golden trout.

Fishing is an art, and a highly skilled scientific sport, he told us, and an adept fisherman can always catch the wily trout but he should do so only when he needs or desires the meat, and never just for sport and never fish just to be fishing. He gave my wife and son good lessons on the tricks of fly fishing, but quickly detected an unteachable pupil in me. Besides being an intractable student, I possess a mite of meanness and occasionally twitted him about my getting a spinning outfit. You may well believe this subject can bring a fine show of sparks to Norman's eyes. I dared not mention bait. But Norman himself was not one hundred percent pure. He seemed to take a chuckling delight in mentioning times when he broke the law. It might have been just a week or two after season and his bag might have been just a few over the limit, and anyway it was way back there on the other side of Mount something-or-other, and he was out of food—is the way he would explain it with another chuckle— and if a game warden was around "he might have arrested me but he'd have eaten the fish too."

Jules will have to tell you of trips in the mountains with Norman and Glen Dawson and climbers of the thirties. I was mostly in Oregon then, and later I was here, but gone on expeditions in the summer. We saw Norman mainly on his one-day-to-three-week periodic visits to our home in Bishop, and on our checkup trips to see him in Big Pine Canyon. Most of our trips then were in winter season and only for a day. Part of the reason for walks in Big Pine Canyon was Norman's aversion at being caught at housekeeping failures. Two or three times in the 1930's, on trips down from Oregon, I had looked up Norman in wintertime and received an invitation to stay in his cluttered up house, but I think he really was apprehensive about my wife seeing him in such disarray. So he would slip out of the cabin as soon as he heard us outside and ask if we wanted to walk. Usually we would walk up the old trail to the "first falls." Naturally Norman would be carrying a rucksack containing two or three cameras, a couple of target pistols with different barrel lengths, spare film, a coat, cup, canteen, and a light lunch. Strapped to his waist he usually wore a .22 Colt Woodsman, and he carried one of his numerous rifles in his hand. I suppose even hand-loaded ammunition was expensive for him, so the rifle was rather seldom used, and it would be leaned up against a convenient Jeffrey pine after an elevation gain of a hundred feet, in order to search the south canyon with binoculars, or else to sit down and wait for the right cloud to hover around the peaks for a proper picture. Including lunch stop, a half day could easily be used up. For Norman, who no doubt made the climb to the top of the first falls almost daily, the walk was a

never-ending delight. He always managed to find something in-
teresting; a bush or a bug, or a cloud shadow on the mountain-
side.

In the 1950's Norman's car was often parked in the field
next to our little house. Somehow it always seemed to fit Norman
perfectly. The old soft top, lashed down with extra straps, the
expanding gate carrier on the running board overflowing with
gear, the tonneau loaded with packs and skis and ropes and ice
axes, all was a perfect match for the driver in his battered
campaign hat. To see him crawl out of the succession of second-
hand disasters he acquired after the old Chev never seemed
right.

Many of the visits to the little house in Bishop were in
springtime, when Norman was, by agreement, cast out of his
mountain cabin at Big Pine Creek, when the proprietors began
their annual cleaning to get ready for fisherman rentals. For
forty years or so Norman really had no permanent year-around
home, as he always had to vacate for the tourist and fishing
season. This suited him in spite of the grumbling about remov-
ing all his valuable collection of shovels and ice axes, his rope-
weaved showshoes, his rusty traps, his more than a score of
large boxes of ancient, squirrel-gnawed classics, his boots and
boot nails and hatchets and saws, the three-foot and five-foot and
seven-foot skis, the boxes and boxes of photographs and writings,
and the twenty tool boxes of handguns he sometimes brought
down to be stored in the valley for greater safety. Everything
else was piled in a great cache in the rocks of the mountainside.
Well, this migration was, as I have mentioned, even earlier than
the actual onset of fishing season because of the time involved
in mucking out the cabin for visitors from the city, so Norman
often came 'round in blustery early spring, suffering from a
cold from having to start his six-month, summer sleeping-out.
He'd chug and sputter up to the house in his old clunker and
announce that on account of old so and so, he had been forced
to vacate a day or three early, and he had a cold already and
he did not get the correct consideration for all the winter's work
he had done, and he really ought to be packing for a trip to the
Rockies and he'd rather go to the Coast Ranges of British
Columbia and he had just bought a fine new "toy," a war sur-
plus Italian army issue carbine of so much horsepower with
eight speeds forward and dual reversing fine tuner, and damna-
tion he had a cold and would have to go to the hospital after a

60

few days at our house resting up. Hospital? Yes, there's a little sun-filled clearing in a grove of white . . . oops, I've almost given it away. Anyhow, in a certain canyon near Bishop is the finest hospital a man could wish for—just a couch of leaves and a clear running stream and soft breezes, and three weeks dozing in the sun under those great cliffs can cure most anything. It is absolutely private and free of cost.

I have just been looking over my copy of Close Ups of the High Sierra, *the book of Norman's writings of 1928 or so. Walt Wheelock says in his brief biography on Norman that "much of the gruffness of his early years has disappeared." This was written about ten years ago and I think there is a continuing mellowness lately in Norman's personality. A few days ago we visited him at the Big Pine Sanitorium where he is residing temporarily, while he can get his cabin refurnished after a looting incident, which left him without lamps for reading or pans for cooking. We asked why he was not up at the old Baker Creek cabin, and Norman explained with such a sudden and loud burst that a passing nurse jumped a foot. The point is, though, in ten seconds Norman was smiling and laughing and saying, "Well, that's the way it goes." There are always gripes, all the time I've known him. Something is always wrong. Often it is his own fault. Even the cop could see that, but he let him go. It was a good story and believable, knowing Norman. He really did leave his driver's license on the stump and the squirrel ate it up.*

I hate to write all these things, in a way. I do not mean to make Norman a buffoon. He was not and is not. It is just that he is so noble that the comic relief is welcome. He laughs at these anecdotes himself. Laughter is one of his notable traits. He laughs often and with gusto and sparkles all around the edges when he gets into a good story, even or especially when the joke is on himself. Yes, he is noble. My wife says, "A gentleman, a thorough and complete gentleman—honest, reliable, dependable, kind, with an old world courtesy." His watch may have stopped and he might have been marking 'x's on last year's calendar, so he'll be a day late but he'll be there.

I mentioned the "hospital." I think Norman very rarely said anything about it. However, he used to be fond of telling everyone about his "hotels." He had hundreds. They were scattered in every corner of the Sierra. A rock ledge, a mossy bench, a hidden tarn. They were isolated, ideal campsites, selected, stocked and used by Norman alone. They were chosen

*for their firewood, water supply and access to climbing routes,
but primarily and almost entirely for their scenic inspiration.
One of the most often-used overlooked the North Palisade group
of peaks, and he called it the Palace Hotel: "The view alone is
worth fifty dollars!"*

*Norman's mountain clothes and gear always interested me
because his reputation required respect for the type of equipment which helped to get him up so many peaks, and because
everything he did had a special Norman Clyde style. Most
notable and identifiable was his trademark, the stiff-brimmed
stetson campaign hat which he wore on every mountain trip.
Even in town, he can be spotted two blocks away by his campaign hat. He must have had a half dozen in the old cabin on
Big Pine Creek one winter I visited him there. I couldn't help
laughing at the oldest. They had spent so many seasons buffeting
up against rocks and bowing into storms and fanning so many
camp fires, that the four-ridged dome had become creased and
broken and he had sewed up the top with white cotton thread,
making a rather ornamental though somewhat ragged pyramid.
Some of the hats were new and apparently used for his rare
visits to the city or even rarer trips to the east coast.*

*Regular climbing pants were not available in this country
in those days, but he manufactured serviceable knickers by
stagging off long trousers and combining them with a unique
gaiter. I think I have never seen such a gaiter anywhere, but it
guarded Norman's legs for a lifetime of climbing. He would
cut off the tops of sixteen-inch boots and install and lace them on
his legs first, and then tie the bottoms into the tops of his regular
six-inch climbing boots to make a firm seal. His climbing boots
followed the regular course of evolution of mountain footwear
from Swiss edge nails through tricouni nails to Bramani soles.
Bramani soles, of course, have completely replaced nails for
American mountaineers, but before their introduction into this
country, Sierran climbers used smooth-soled rubber, and north-
westerners with their icy mountains more often used nails. Norman carried both. Two sets of boots, and with skis he carried
another pair to fit the bindings.*

*Norman's ideas on equipment were heavy but practical. I
often imitated him. As late as 1953, to my partner Gary Leech's
consternation, I carried two boots on an ascent of the North
Palisade. As Norman said, "For secure footing—rubber on
rock, steel on ice." Which reminds me I was still using some of*

Norman's heavy gear on my first big expedition to Alaska in the 1950's. I picked up his habit of using a Yukon packboard with a lashed on duffel bag, and maybe that was the year I first saw a strange new thing called a Kelty pack. Anyway, Norman's six-pound packboard proved rugged and strong enough to survive a flub-dub crevasse mishap when my partner's lesser packboard collapsed.

Is it any part of a mountaineer's life how he conducts himself in town? Perhaps. Actually there's little to report here, except that Norman is not an uncommon sight in Bishop. He comes to town in recent months quite regularly, about once a fortnight, parks his old car in front of our house and walks Main Street for "raids on the ten-cent store," and visits to the secondhand store, the current church rummage sale, maybe a check-in with the sheriff's office to moan about the latest vandalism at Baker Creek Ranch. Might be he would stop in at the Forest Service and get involved in "one of my tomfool stories about life in the mountains during the eocene era," and most important—a sortie to the grocery store to lay in a supply for the old cabin. This is quite a contrast, come to think about it, to the old days on Big Pine Creek when he sometimes came to town so seldom that he nearly lost the power of speech. Well, lately he comes to get some home cooking and how he does love to talk. Walt Wheelock called him "taciturn." Does Walt really know Norman? Maybe a long time ago, but today he is no total stranger and many recognize the slightly stooped figure, slowed but little by his eighty-six years, always crowned with the stetson, a rucksack on his back and a sagging brief case in his hand.

63

"Such an aerie would have been chosen as his final resting place by this departed lover of the mountains."

The Quest for Walter A. Starr, Jr.

WALTER A. STARR, JR., an attorney from San Francisco, was in many respects a remarkable young man. Not only did he possess unusual ability in his chosen profession, but he had already given evidence of considerable literary and musical talent. His character was in every way exemplary. He was also very fond of the outdoors, especially of the high mountains, most of all the Sierra Nevada. This love for the outdoors was in part purely esthetic, in part joy in thrilling adventures to be had in exploration, and still more in mountain climbing. Therefore, whenever time was available, he rambled away to the high mountains, often on solitary trips. While on one of these in 1933, he had an appointment to meet his parents during the first week of August. Day after day passed, however, without his appearing. About a week later the news reached me while on a climbing trip.

"Strange," I thought. "Being such a man as he is, he would keep his appointment—unless something unusual has happened."

Several days later word came that his deserted camp had been found at Lake Ediza. "The Minarets," I reflected.

A day later I was riding through the mountains to the place of rendezvous—Lake Ediza. Upon reaching it, I found that a party of about twenty had already assembled, including volunteer friends from San Francisco and Los Angeles, representatives of the Forest Service and the California State Highway Patrol, together with Walter A. Starr, Sr. Among them were a half-dozen trained mountain climbers.

A plan of procedure was quickly formed. In the vicinity stand two high mountains, Mt. Ritter and Banner Peak, with summits averaging slightly over 13,000 feet. South of them a short distance stand a long crescent-like line of jagged spires averaging some 12,000 feet in elevation, and several miles in length from the northwest to the southeast. These are very appropriately called The Minarets.

Almost undoubtedly Walter Starr had met with mishap somewhere in this group of mountains, the Ritter Range, and was either somewhere on them or in the country lying between them and his camp. If killed or seriously injured he was probably in the mountains, but if he were only crippled he might have attempted to reach camp and, being unable to do so, would be in the lower country. A man with a sprained ankle or broken leg may spend days in going a short distance. The plan of campaign was based on these facts. Those without special mountaineering experience were to comb the area lying between his camp and the base of the Ritter Range. The mountaineers were to search the peaks and spires, a difficult, arduous, and somewhat hazardous undertaking.

Early the next morning four climbing parties were on their way. Three excellent young climbers, Jules Eichorn, of San Francisco, together with Glen Dawson and Richard Jones of Los Angeles, proceeded to search one portion of the Minarets, especially the second-highest—Michael's Minaret—while Oliver Kehrlein of Oakland and I were to direct our efforts to another section of the great spires, focusing upon the highest of them, known as Clyde's Minaret.

Past a number of groves of mountain hemlocks, and through gradually rising alpine meadows we filed along to the glaciated bluffs immediately below the Minarets. Along these cliffs Kehrlein and I proceeded, carefully inspecting every foot of the way until we were abreast of the highest of the Minarets. Aside from a few footprints which might have been those of a party other than the one for whom we were searching, we discovered nothing. Unfortunately we did not know the pattern of the soles of the basketball shoes generally worn by the missing man when rock climbing.

Leaving the bluffs, we crossed a small but rather steeply pitching glacier to the base of Clyde's Minaret and continued up its precipitous north face. More tracks were observed in the decomposed granite on the ledges, but these also were in all likelihood those of another party. Upon reaching the jagged top of the great spire, the signature of Walter Starr was not in the register in the cairn. However, we knew that he did not always sign his name on the top of a mountain, and furthermore there was no pencil in the register can and he might have failed to bring one with him. No evidence of his having been there was discovered.

As we looked out over the mountains an inky mass of clouds was seen advancing from the southwest and another from the northeast. As the top of a pinnacle more than 12,000 feet above the sea is not the most desirable place to encounter an electric storm, we left the summit before we had searched it to our entire satisfaction. On our way down we zigzagged back and forth, minutely observing every square yard for clues, but none were found.

When we reached the glacier, I swung around a promontory and found a long ledge running across the northeast face of the peak. Knowing the adventurous character of the lost man, I had a strong suspicion that he would attempt this apparently sheer, and so far as we knew, hitherto unscaled front of the mountain. About midway across the latter I came upon a "duck" —a small heap of rocks, usually pyramidal in form, erected as a marker to indicate a route followed. Presently I saw another and then a whole line of them leading to the head of a steep chimney on the southeast shoulder of the mountain. The ducks had evidently been constructed no great while before, as some of them were so unstable that they would have toppled over under the first heavy wind. However, it did not seem very likely that Starr would have approached this face from the southeast, and we knew that another party, of whose movements we had not been informed, had also been in this vicinity. Later we learned that such a party had recently made an unsuccessful attempt to scale the Minaret by this route.

As it was now late afternoon we were obliged to return. While doing so we paused and reconnoitered on the margin of Upper Iceberg Lake, lying on Minaret Pass a short distance northeast of Clyde's Minaret at an elevation of some 10,000 feet. We thought Starr might have passed this lake on his way to the mountain. While looking about, I noticed a strip of handkerchief with blood marks on it.

"Someone has lost his footing and cut his finger on a sharp rock as he came up the steep slope to the north of the pass," I thought as I stowed it away in my rucksack.

Upon our return to camp we found that the large party had come upon no certain evidence of any kind in the lower country. During the day an aeroplane carrying Francis P. Farquhar, President of the Sierra Club, as observer, had circled the peaks of the Ritter Range several times, evidently without result.

Walter A. Starr, Sr. and his son Allan had climbed Banner Peak and searched the North Glacier in descending, but found no record on the summit. Two, however, who had climbed Mt. Ritter, Douglas Robinson, Jr., and Lilburn Norris, discovered that Starr had written a note in the register on its summit. Among several statements was one to the effect that he had his ice axe with him. The latter having been found at his camp was proof of his safe return from Mt. Ritter. The other Minaret party which had climbed Michael's Minaret from the west, saw a line of ducks similar to those encountered by us. The markers crossed the upper end of a chute and led to "The Portal" on the north side of Michael's Minaret. There were also several footprints and a portion of a cigarette, which was said to be the brand usually smoked by the missing man. Eichorn and Dawson had climbed from "The Portal" to the summit of the Minaret but found no evidence of Starr having been there, and were forced to make a hurried descent by the same storm that drove me from Clyde's Minaret. By its brown marking the fragment of the handkerchief which I had brought in was identified as similar to those generally carried by Starr.

Haunted by the ducks on the northeast face of Clyde's Minaret, Kehrlein and I returned on the following morning to Upper Iceberg Lake. Swinging around to the slope east of it, we selected a vantage point from which the entire northeast face could be readily surveyed with binoculars. An object about a third of the way up the mountain puzzled me. The fact that it was brown indicated that it might be a khaki-clad person, but as the light falling upon it seemed to be diffused through it rather than reflected from it, this inference seemed to be precluded.

Having come to the decision that this face of the peak should be thoroughly investigated, we proceeded to climb it. In about half an hour we reached the long ledge. After examining several ducks, I carefully removed the rocks of one of them. Beneath was a tuft of grass the color of which had not faded in the least. This was certain proof that the ducks had been made very recently. As we began to advance up the peak we presently came upon more ducks. Then there was a gap. Evidently the climber was in the habit of putting markers only when he thought that there might be special occasion for them on his return. A little later we reached the object which had aroused our curiosity. It was a bed of oxalis, or miner's lettuce, a few feet in length on a ledge, with a profusion of brown seed vessels; both the color and the diffusion of light were therefore explained.

The ducks appeared to lead into a large alcove-like recess

in a chute or couloir, with almost vertical walls of perhaps a hundred feet above it. Then they were lost again. Working my way upward along narrow shelves, I succeeded in getting within a few yards of the rim of the wall, but the remainder being very hazardous, I desisted from the attempt to scale it. While traversing to the right along ledges toward the rib of rock separating this couloir from another adjoining it to the north, I again came upon ducks. There was one on the very crest of the rib and others in the next chute. I called down to Kehrlein. In a few minutes he joined me.

Together we proceeded up the couloir. Although the line of ducks was not continuous, there were sufficient to indicate clearly the route taken by the climber. As we neared the head of the couloir, an approaching mass of dense black cloud, together with thunder in the distance, warned us that we had better get off the precipitous face. The rocks were difficult enough to scale when dry, and furthermore, a storm striking the pinnacle would be likely to precipitate loose ones down upon us. (Starr's name was found the following year by Jules Eichorn on the summit of the Minaret, faintly marked on a piece of cardboard. Starr's diary subsequently proved that the ducks we followed marked his route.)

When we reached the foot of the peak, several hours of daylight still remaining, we proceeded southward around the base. We had not gone far before we observed Eichorn and his party coming from the opposite direction, making their way down a steep couloir. Confronted by a vertical drop of perhaps fifty feet, capped by a great stone, they spent some little time in looking about for a rock to which a rope might be safely attached. Eventually finding one, they were presently seen gliding in turn down the double rope, which the last man pulled down after him. A short time later they joined us. They had found ducks leading up the second chute north of Michael's chimney which eventually connected with the ducks seen by them before, leading along the arête to the pinnacle of Michael's Minaret. The ducks had been recently placed by an experienced route-finder as indicated by the excellence of the route chosen. Having climbed to the summit of Michael's Minaret from this position the day before, they had climbed the third-highest, Eichorn's Minaret, on which they hoped some evidence would be discovered. Disappointed in this, they had descended and had gone around Michael's Minaret and climbed a considerable distance up the southwest face of Clyde's Minaret and then passed through a notch to the side on which we were.

When we reached camp late in the evening we found that the large party had come to the conclusion that there was little or no possibility of finding Starr in the territory which they had carefully searched, and had, therefore, left the mountains. At a round table of the mountaineering parties, after considerable discussion, it was decided that it would be well to investigate the east face of Banner Peak, as there is a dangerous and only once-traveled route up it, which, it was thought, might have enticed the missing man to attempt it.

On the ensuing morning, therefore, we walked several miles northwestward to the east base of Banner Peak. After going slowly and carefully along this without finding any evidence, the party divided, Eichorn and his two companions proceeding up the lower portion of the route in question, while Kehrlein and I swung around a rock promontory onto a glacier, from which we could command the northeast face immediately below the route. Several hours of searching by both parties indicated that Starr had not attempted to scale this face of Banner Peak. We therefore returned to camp.

At another round table that evening, after an animated debate, it was decided that further search would almost undoubtedly prove futile, and it would be best to give it up. To find a person in such a maze of pinnacles, only a few of which had been scaled, was like finding a needle in a haystack, it was thought. Not yet ready to abandon the quest, however, I declined to accompany the remainder of the party.

On the following morning I set forth on my lone quest. There is another Minaret—Leonard's—climbed but once prior to that year, which it seemed possible that Starr might have attempted to scale. It might be well, therefore, to ascend this, and incidentally to ascertain whether the missing man had gone north of Michael's Notch. In a word, my plan was to be one of gradual elimination. As now there was no further hope of finding Starr alive, there was no special occasion for hurry.

Through the alpine meadows, already beginning to show signs of the approach of autumn, and over the bluffs I picked my way to a glacier beneath the north face of the spire which I wished to scale. After examining it carefully, I crossed the glacier and climbed a short distance to a wide notch. From this I followed a narrow knife edge, involving some rather difficult and dangerous climbing, to the top of the spire. However, no one had recently been there. While carefully sweeping the Minarets with my binoculars—as I did a score of times daily—I trained them on the northwest face of Michael's Minaret.

"A capital place for a fall," I reflected, as I thrust my glasses into a pocket of my rucksack.

Upon reaching the wide notch again, I decided to go down to the west base and follow it until abreast of Michael's Notch, a cleft about a third of the way southward along the sweeping crescent described by the Minarets. I carefully examined every foot of terrain over which I passed, without, however, finding a single indication of anyone having gone that way. Passing through the notch to the opposite side of the Minarets, I returned to camp. Starr, I felt certain, had not been north of Michael's Notch. This was step number one in my plan of elimination.

I was not yet entirely satisfied as to Clyde's Minaret. Almost without doubt Walter Starr had climbed it, or at least had attempted to do so. This was indicated both by the line of ducks on the peak and by the fragment of handkerchief found on the margin of Upper Iceberg Lake. He was also reported as having said that he contemplated bivouacing at this lake the night preceeding a proposed ascent of Clyde's Minaret.

With these things in mind, I therefore went again to the lake. Despite careful search, however, nothing further was observed until the south end of the lake was reached. There I found footprints, and recent ones at that, in the granite sand. The imprints indicated a shoe larger than that worn by the missing man and of a type not used by him when on rock climbs. As the person who made them seemed to have come up Minaret Creek from the South, I went down over cliffs to Minaret Lake. There horse tracks were found. Evidently a forest ranger or a sheep man had come up the stream. This day's search therefore added nothing to my stock of information.

As human muscles have a habit of eventually clamoring for rest, after climbing and searching for an average of at least ten hours daily for five days, I thought it might be well to accede to their demand by spending a day in camp. On the following day, the twenty-first of August, I decided to settle, if possible, the matter of Clyde's Minaret. Returning to the northeast face, I again followed the line of ducks up its precipitous front. They ceased entirely at the head of the couloir up which Kehrlein and I had followed them on the previous climb. Con-

71

tinuing to the summit, I inspected cairn and rocks very carefully without finding any certain evidence. Barring the possibility of his having been forced back by a storm, however, I felt convinced that Starr had been there.

In the descent I swung in long zigzags back and forth across the northeast and north faces. At the base of the latter lies a glacier, and along its upper margin runs a deep bergschrund. One of the theories of the disappearance of Starr was to the effect that he had fallen into this crevasse. As I rounded the glacier the light happened to fall at such an agle that I could inspect the bottom of the bergschrund through almost the entire length. The fact that nothing was seen did not, however, prove that Starr had not fallen into it, for snow cornices were frequently collapsing into it, and rocks, including small slides, often rattled down the face of the mountain, for the most part plunging into it.

Several other considerations, however, were almost conclusive that he had not gone into the crevasse. In the first place, Starr was a climber of such skill that he would not be likely to suffer a fall on this face, a considerably easier one than the northeastern which he had evidently scaled. Secondly, a person would not, in all likelihood, have been precipitated any great distance down the face of the mountain without leaving some evidence in the form of clothing, rucksack, or other personal belongings on the ledges with which it is seamed. I had so carecully scrutinized these that even a chipmunk exposed on them could scarcely have escaped my detection. In the third place, had a person fallen down the face of the mountain, there was a fair likelihood that either he or some of his effects would have jumped the crevasse and remained lying on the surface of the glacier. Assessing the evidence, both positive and negative, I returned to camp convinced that Walter Starr had climbed Clyde's Minaret, or had attempted to do so and had been driven back by storm, but that in either case he had returned to camp without mishap. The Minaret was therefore eliminated from further consideration.

On the ensuing day the search was primarily a binocular one. Beyond Minaret Pass I continued southward, eventually traversing a glacier and crossing a pass to the southwestern side of the Minarets. From various vantage points I carefully and repeatedly swept the entire reach of cliffs, including the east front of Michael's Minaret, which thrusts out about midway along the crescent formed by this line of great spires, without, however, detecting a single bit of evidence of any kind. On my return I scaled an outlying Minaret and repeated the procedure, with a like result.

After returning to camp, I summed up the evidence as follows: In the limited time at his disposal, Starr would in all probability not have attempted to scale more than Clyde's and Michael's Minarets. There was no indication of his having been any distant southeast of the former, or of his having been north of Michael's Notch. He had obviously climbed, or attempted to climb, Clyde's Minaret, but after most careful search, there was no reason to believe that he had not returned safely to camp. There remained Michael's Minaret. I decided to rest a day in camp and then attempt it.

Early in the morning of the twenty-fifth I again traversed the alpine meadows, again clambered up on the glaciated bluffs and then continued up a long slanting ledge ending in a short chimney, out of the upper end of which I climbed into Michael's Notch. From it an easy descent brought me to the west base of the Minarets. I then went southward about a mile to the west side of Michael's Minaret and continued around its southwestern shoulder. Noting a shelf running along the precipitous— almost sheer—west face, I decided to follow it for some distance and then climb above it in order to get a vantage point suitable for using my binoculars.

While reconnoitering, I came to the conclusion that higher up probably a ledge would be found leading around this shoulder and into the upper portion of a deep chute to "The Portal", from which the final spire of the Minaret is usually scaled. While I advanced upward the climbing became rather delicate, as the holds grew progressively smaller. They were firm and sharp angled, however, and there was no occasion to worry about loose rocks—the face was too steep for rocks to find lodgement.

As anticipated, a ledge did lead into the couloir. After going some distance up the latter, I examined the northwestern face of the spire. Evidently it was scalable, but the ledges tended to slope downward at a precarious angle, and there was a predominance of rounded corners. Knowing Starr's reliance on rubber-soled shoes, I made a mental comment to the effect that this reliance was perhaps a little too great. After climbing it for some distance I suddenly made the decision:

"This can be climbed, but I am not going to do it."

Having returned to the couloir, I continued up it to the notch ("The Portal") at its head. The ascent of perhaps five hundred feet from it to the narrow, blade-like summit of the spire involved a good deal of aerial and some rather hazardous climbing. Seated on the topmost rock, several feet in diameter, for upwards of a half hour, I swept the Minaret with my binoculars. Gathering clouds then warned me that I had better be gone.

As I carefully and deliberately made my way down toward the notch, I scanned and re-scanned the northwestern face. Much of it was concealed by irregularities. Suddenly a fly droned past, then another, and another.

"The quest is nearing an end," I reflected.

Upon reaching "The Portal" I began to follow a ledge running in a northwesterly direction. When I had gone along it but a few yards, turning about, I looked upward and across the chute to the northwestern face. There, lying on a ledge not more than fifty yards distant, were the earthly remains of Walter A. Starr, Jr. He had obviously fallen, perhaps several hundred feet, to instantaneous death. The quest had been long, arduous, and hazardous, but the mystery of the vanishing of Walter Starr, Jr. was at last solved. The life of the daring young climber had come to a sudden and tragic end.

A few days later a party of four was again scaling Michael's Minaret. We followed the route which Starr had marked with ducks while making his climb three weeks before. Several hundred feet below the remains, two stopped, but Jules Eichorn and I continued up the perilous face. We interred the body of Walter A. Starr, Jr. on the narrow ledge where it lay, while his father looked up from below. Such an aerie would have been chosen as his final resting place by this departed lover of the mountains.

An Early Ascent of the East Face
of Bear Creek Spire

D URING THE SECOND WEEK of
July now a considerable number of years ago, three of us—Hervey Voge, Dave Brower, and myself—set forth early one morning from our camp along the margin of a lake at the northern end of Little Lakes Basin on the headwaters of Rock Creek, having as our goal for the day an ascent of Bear Creek Spire. Little Lakes Basin is oval in form, several miles in length, and its undulating floor, lying in the zone immediately below timberline, is sown with several score of lakes varying from miniature tarns across which one might toss a stone to lakes a quarter of a mile or more in length. Except to the north it is surrounded by an imposing array of high peaks, four of which attain elevations of more than 13,700 feet. The most spectacular although not the highest of these is Bear Creek Spire, which looks down into a large cirque on the headwaters of Rock Creek. In form it is what geologists term a Matterhorn or simply "horn." Four glaciers working from as many directions gradually carved back the original mass of the mountain, until, assisted by other weathering agencies, especially by the rending action of frost, the mountain eventually assumed the striking type of peak which we see today. Although it affords a number of routes involving climbing sufficiently interesting to entice the mountaineer, at the time which I have in mind it had been ascended but seldom and in the matter of negotiable routes was not beyond the exploratory stage.

As we headed southward, following an abandoned mining road, it was a delightful morning with cloudless sky and bright sunshine—typical of mid-summer in the high Sierra. Scarcely a breeze stirred the azure lakes which we skirted, or rustled the boughs of lodgepole and whitebark pines. The spectacular pyramidal form of Bear Creek Spire, a few miles distant, looked down into the head of the canyon.

At an altitude of some 11,000 feet the undulating floor of the basin began to rise rather rapidly. Leaving the road as it swung to the east, we continued southward, roughly following the course of the stream at first through an open stand of pines.

75

As the elevation gradually increased and the terrain became rougher, the trees decreased in number and size until, at a cluster of beautiful sapphire lakes (lying at an elevation of some 11,500 feet) we passed the last sizeable ones.

For some distance, however, we continued to traverse small alpine meadows. About mid-July in normal years in the high Sierra, the alpine flowers have almost reached their climax. On the meadows we noticed considerable numbers of the diminutive vaccinium or dwarf bilberry, with pendent pure white and pink flowers. On the moister portions of the meadows, the kalmia or mountain laurel displayed clusters of pink, drooping, small rhododendron-like blossoms. Its larger relative, the *bryanthus* or red heather, displayed masses of rose-purple, spicily fragrant flowers. On the talus slopes lying along the bases of the bluffs, graceful columbine—white, orange and red—seemed to float in the air, swaying back and forth in the slightest breeze. As we emerged from the upper end of the canyon into the cirque lying at its head and still in large measure covered with snow, we frequently came upon the bright flowers of the draba, an extremely hardy little alpine plant which grew in the areas free of snow.

Bear Creek Spire's sheer north face looks down into the cirque. We wished, however, to scale its precipitous eastern face, so we crossed a col or saddle with an elevation of some 12,500 feet to the headwaters of Morgan Creek, directly east of Bear Creek Spire. The east face was then directly west of us. From the summit of the mountain two narrow dentated arêtes descend, one in a southeasterly direction to the south of the cirque at the head of Morgan Creek; the other, in a northeasterly direction down to the col which we had crossed. The general course of the route we wished to follow lay a short distance to the right of the latter. We crossed the cirque and began to ascend a narrow ridge leading toward it.

Here our first real climbing began. We scaled a rather precipitous buttress to the left of a snow- and ice-filled couloir several hundred feet in height. At the head of the latter we swung abruptly to the right and began to ascend obliquely across a number of couloirs separated by sharp ribs. Due to foreshortening, the portion of the face of the mountain which we were now attacking had appeared almost unscalable from a distance; now, however, we found it to be what mountaineers term only interestingly difficult. The steeply inclining floors of the couloirs did require care, and now and then we came upon a pitch which called for the use of gymnastics. The lower ends of the couloirs terminated in a tier of cliffs which we had flanked by going to the left, but a glissade down any of the couloirs would have carried us over the edge, where we would have needed a parachute, but had none.

In about a hundred feet of almost vertical rise we reached the upper end of a couloir. Above us about 500 feet of precipitous face rose to the blade-like summit of the mountain. Up this we continued diagonally, picking our way along ledges, and hoisting ourselves over steep intervening pitches. Eventually we climbed directly upward to what appeared to be the highest point of the top of the mountain. Somewhat to our surprise we found ourselves on the crest only a few yards from the base of a rounded monolith at its southern end, the top of which is the true summit, 13,705 feet above the sea.

The final monolith of Bear Creek Spire is a short but somewhat difficult escalade. From a notch in the crest at its northern base one swings his right foot well up to a cup-like cavity, and then works his way upward as best he may, chiefly by friction, over a rounded shoulder to the top of the rock only a few feet in diameter. To the southeast the mountain falls away sheer for a long distance to the headwaters of Pine Creek. This is in fact one of the most aerial perches of the higher summits of the Sierra.

The view obtained from it is magnificent, extending from Mt. Whitney some fifty miles to the south to the mountains of Yosemite Park about an equal distance in the opposite direction. As already mentioned, Bear Creek Spire is a Matterhorn-type mountain. From a cirque at its eastern base Morgan Creek flows eastward, with Mt. Morgan, highest peak in the area with an altitude of 13,748 feet, to the north. To the northeast lies the amphitheatre on the headwaters of Pine Creek, with the rounded, pleasingly colored pyramid of Mt. Tom southeastward across the profound canyon of Pine Creek. Immediately west of the peak lies Italy Basin almost entirely above timberline with Mt. Abbot (13,715 feet) and Mt. Dade (13,600) at its head and Mts. Gabb and Hilgard hemming it in to the west. To the north runs Rock Creek with Mt. Morgan to the east; Mts. Dade, Abbot, and Mills to the west. It was a perfect day on the mountain top, with a cloudless azure sky overarching the vast panorama of mountain, valley and desert. Scarcely a breeze stirred and the sunshine fell warm on the narrow blade-like summit, as we leisurely ate luncheon, reclining on the sun-warmed rocks.

In the descent we followed the crest of the northeastern arête for a short distance, but soon this became so jagged that we abandoned it in favor of ledges running along its south face. A few hundred feet farther down, however, we swung back again to the crest of the arête. Our progress downward then became pleasantly interesting as we picked our way along the crest down over pitches, over or around pinnacles, or along ledges running along the south face.

As we neared the base of the mountain we came upon an abrupt drop-off. Down its front ran a number of chimneys—one might perhaps rather call them large crevices. Holds were none too numerous but when these were inadequate we succeeded in making our way down them by wedging ourselves into the available space. Several hundred feet of easy descent then brought us to the lower end of the arête and the col immediately below it. From this we descended northward to the headwaters of Rock Creek down which we followed the route which we had used in the morning.

The western half of canyon and basin below it now lay in deep shadow; the eastern half, in bright sunlight. When we were well down the canyon we halted and looked back to Bear Creek Spire towering above the cirque. Brilliant rays of evening sunshine streamed across its sheer pyramidal front surmounted by the sharp summit; the lower portion of the mountain lay buried in dark shadow. Farther down we halted again, and as we looked back the summit of Bear Creek Spire glowed roseate in the last rays of setting sun, the end of a perfect day in the high Sierra.

Up the North Face of Mt. Humphreys

OFTEN I HAD LOOKED up the precipitous north face of Mt. Humphreys, an exceptionally rugged peak in the southern Sierra Nevada with a summit of 13,986 feet in altitude, speculating as to whether it might be possible to climb it. On the preceeding day I had knapsacked up a steep canyon to timberline, here an elevation of some 11,000 feet, where I made camp. This morning, thinking it wise to climb the first peak to the north in order to survey the north face of Mt. Humphreys, I was preparing to do so, when, carefully scanning Mt. Humphreys' north face with my binoculars I observed two places where the apparently sheer rock was broken into ledges and chimneys which might permit its ascent, and changed my mind.

"*Carpe diem,*" I thought, "Tomorrow it may be storming and a few inches of snow on the ledges will render the scaling of the face of the mountain unduly hazardous, if not actually impossible."

Swinging my rucksack to my back and picking up my ice axe, I strode down through a scattering of whitebark pines to the margin of a small lake. After crossing the outlet and skirting its lower margin, I trudged up a steep slope for some distance and then made my way over loose moraine, heaped unusually high, to the margin of a small glacier. This traversed, I came to the lower end of a steep couloir or gully leading up to the sharp, cleaver-like crest which runs eastward from the top of Mt. Humphreys.

To avoid cutting steps in the flinty ice on the floor of this chute, I climbed the wall to the left of it for some distance and then began to follow a narrow and nearly horizontal ledge. Presently this almost vanished, and what was left of it was covered with loose rocks. Some of this I cleared away with my ice axe, the rocks bounding down the cliff to the glacier, but while looking ahead I inadvertently placed my hand on a rock of considerable size, so delicately balanced that a few seconds of pressure caused it to totter. Letting go, in a split second I threw my weight forward and swung past it. An instant of delay and I should probably have accompanied the rock in a wild course down the steep drop and out onto the glacier. Although the mountaineer is usually careful to avoid such possibilities, with the best of precautions they sometimes occur. When they do happen it is often so rapidly that, like the soldier with the bullet that is past, he pays little heed to them. They are over so quickly that he scarcely has time to become alarmed.

The end of the almost-vanished ledge reached, I crossed the couloir and clambered upward to the terminal of a wide shelf running obliquely upward across the face of Mt. Humphreys. Once before I had climbed to the top of a mass of loosely staggered rocks to reconnoiter this part of the route when suddenly a ton or more of them had given way and gone crashing over the cliff to the glacier several hundred feet below. Fortunately, anticipating such a contingency, I had taken the precaution of having two good handholds on firm rock above and, aside from the embarrassment of dangling in space for a few moments, I had suffered no harm. That had been in early summer when the ledge was covered with snow as were most of the others over the entire face of the mountain. In addition to the difficulty of scaling the peak in such conditions, I knew that later in the day, as the snow would begin to thaw, at least an occasional rock would come ricocheting down with a report like a rifle shot at every bound. Although not over-endowed with precaution, I did not consider it expedient to attempt to scale the north face then. Only in late summer and early autumn, with the rocks almost free from snow, could the ascent be made without incurring hazard.

As it was now the middle of September, most of the snow had disappeared, including that of the first fall of the season. However, traversing the shelf, although in most places it was broad, was not unattended with difficulty and danger. Loose debris covered it and, the whole sloping at an unsafe angle, it was necessary to exercise extreme care to avoid being carried over the outer rim by a sudden slide of rocks. Within a short distance the shelf narrowed as it swung around a buttress at the base of which loose rocks were heaped up several feet high. A slight pull with my ice axe sent one weighing hundreds of pounds careening down the precipice. Realizing that, should I attempt to cross these rocks I should in all probability go blithely over the crags and land in another world, I set about clearing them with my ice axe. After dislodging what seemed

80

tons of them, hugging the wall I got around the buttress. Beyond this I picked my way over and around other rocks not quite so unstable, with the exception of one slab poised horizontally above me so delicately that a mere touch caused it to sway.

The loose rock was presently followed by wet gravel frozen hard and inclining at a disconcerting angle. Since it was difficult to cut steps in this material and the soft edgenails of my boots did not hold any too firmly to it, as soon as possible I abandoned the wide shelf for narrow but comparatively safe ledges on the rock wall above it. A good ledge but a few inches wide may be much less hazardous than a broad but treacherous shelf such as I had been following.

These narrow ledges, zigzagging back and forth, led me over a spur and down to a wide and rather steep shelf beyond. Fortunately this was almost entirely free from loose material. As I made my way along it, the face of the mountain above became more and more broken into ledges. I cut upward, at first over steeply inclined slabby rock with holds none too numerous or commodious. Here and there the rock was coated with ice several inches thick.

After picking my way back and forth for some distance up this steep slabby rock, I hoisted myself from it to the end of a ledge, or rather one of a series running diagonally upward and to the left. Except for occasional steep pitches, the going here was less difficult. If one ledge became undesirably difficult, I could usually clamber up to the next one above it. Once, however, in attempting to do so, I was confronted by a large rock lodged in a short chimney which had many other rocks resting on it. This rock, I observed, was securely anchored at one end but the other looked a bit dubious. If it were not firmly locked, even the weight of a person might dislodge the whole mass. I therefore swung carefully around rather than over it. From ledge to ledge, over pitch after pitch I thus made my way upward for hundreds of feet. Eventually I pulled myself up onto the crest or arête which, like the upturned edge of a huge wedge, rose westward to the top of the mountain, still about a thousand feet above me.

Although I had surmounted the north face, there were still difficulties ahead. I had gained the crest at the base of a steep step in it. On my first attempt to scale the peak by following this, it had given me trouble; in fact, it had frustrated that attempt to make my ascent. On my next try, however, I found that the

obstruction could be flanked by following a narrow ledge leading to the left part way around a buttress. At the end of this I
slithered down to a rock lodged, apparently none too firmly, in
the head of a chimney that cuts a furrow in the north face of the
mountain and falls away sheer for a thousand feet or more.
Beyond this there was a sheer drop of a thousand feet and above
it a steep face cut by a number of deep, crevice-like grooves
running up to the crest at a point immediately above the step.

On the several previous occasions on which I had gone up
this steep pitch I had removed my rucksack and tied it, together
with my ice axe, to one end of a 100 foot alpine rope, the
other end attached about my waist. This left me unencumbered
during the escalade, but the rock was such that it was difficult
to haul up the rucksack after the crest had been reached. In fact,
once while doing this, standing on a narrow blade of rock with
my left foot resting on an apparently stable knot, when I had
thrown my weight on it while tugging on the rope, the knob had
suddenly given way. Losing my balance, I fell, but luckily
across rather than off the blade—otherwise I should have made
a very hurried trip down the almost vertical face of the mountain.

On the present ascent, therefore, I decided to carry all my
impedimenta with me. Halfway up the pitch, with hands and
feet wedged in two adjoining crevices, the weight of my rucksack pulling outward and my ice axe dangling sword-fashion
from my belt, I rather regretted my decision. However, a perch
in such position is not a very good place to change one's mind,
so I laboriously hitched and hoisted myself up to the crest.

For several hundred yards the gradually rising arête was
broken into pinnacles—gendarmes, mountaineers would call
them—which I sometimes went directly over, by a frontal attack as it were, and sometimes flanked by following ledges cut
into their steep walls. There was one ledge, the only feasible one
on that pinnacle, which ran underneath an overhang so that I
was obliged to edge along in a more or less doubled over position.

This dentated stretch of crest traversed, I came upon a
fragment of summit plateau, as the geologists term a remnant of
an ancient landscape dating back millions of years but remaining
comparatively unchanged while the surrounding terrain had
been slowly carved into precipitous crags and pinnacles by the
various eroding agencies. The gradual slope of this summit

plateau is topped by a false summit, separated from the true one several hundred feet higher by a shallow notch at the head of a great chute running down the southwestern face of the mountain. The final pinnacle looked formidable, but from previous experience I knew it to be scalable without any very great difficulty.

After picking my way for a short distance up over slabby rocks, I came upon a sort of chimney. In this I was presently halted by an overhanging rock. Although I could reach over it, to pull myself over it by main force would involve a rather arduous lift. There seemed to be an alternative in swinging around and upward to some grooves in the steeply pitching rock. A sliver wedged in a crevice seemed to afford a good handhold for such a purpose. "It might break off beneath my weight," I thought as I examined it. In mountain climbing sometimes slight precautions spell the difference between safety and disaster. Finding a higher and better hand-, or rather arm hold, I succeeded in swinging myself up and around the obstruction. In a few minutes I stood on the top of the mountain, a mass of shattered rock a few yards in diameter and 13,986 feet above the sea.

Extending as it does from Mt. Whitney, sixty miles in an air-line to the south and slightly westward, to the mountains of Yosemite about an equal distance away, the view obtained from the top of Mt. Humphreys is one of the finest in the Sierra Nevada. To the east the range drops away abruptly in a great escarpment cut by numerous deep gorges to the floor of Owens Valley, in places 10,000 feet below the crest of the Sierra. To the west, rent here and there by great canyons, it sweeps gradually down to the broad valley of the San Joaquin River.

A dozen times or more I had stood or sat on this narrow summit. Once while reclining against the cairn, I suddenly heard a rushing sound. As I turned in its direction a golden eagle swooped past, almost within arm's length. Evidently intending to alight on the monument, it had not observed me until within a few yards. After swooping downward for perhaps a thousand feet, it swung upward and was soon calmly soaring about in the blue sky. A similar incident occurred to me on the summit of Mt. Winchell, a sharp peak some twenty miles south of Mt. Humphreys. Eagles are fond of perching on such peaks of the Sierra. I sat eating my luncheon on the mountain top, watching the rosy finches flit from rock to rock. The sight of this cheery and confiding little bird on the summits of the mountains of the West is always welcome to the mountaineer.

Since it was mid-afternoon, I could not tarry long. I was soon on my down the west face of the peak, following the route by which the first ascent of the mountain had been made in 1904 by the Hutchinson brothers, members of the Sierra Club. Like most mountains of any great difficulty, Mt. Humphreys was at first regarded as impossible of ascent and, after being climbed for the first time, was looked upon for a number of years as a "one way" mountain. Eventually, however, upwards of a half dozen routes were found leading to the summit from all sides. This ascent was the first occasion on which the precipitous north face had been scaled.

The route led down a narrow knife edge which fell away sharply on either side. After following the rather airy crest for a few rods, I swung over a steep drop, the holds being excellent so that there was no occasion for alarm. Letting myself down a steep wall, I swung around the end of it to the head of a steep chute. By this time I had descended about two hundred and fifty feet. An equal distance farther down the floor and sides of a chute, I came to the Married Men's Monument. This is a large cairn said to have been erected by the married men of an early climbing party who, evidently not relishing the looks of the final pyramid, used their family responsibilities as sufficient reason for not proceeding farther. While awaiting the return of their carefree companions they are reputed to have built this monument.

After passing through a notch, I came to the head of a steep couloir or chute running down the northeastern face of the mountain. To the right it was flanked by sheer crags, but to the left were cliffs sufficiently broken by ledges to render them only moderately difficult to descend. At the foot of the cliffs I came to the margin of a glacier at a point where, on a previous occasion, I had leaped the uppermost crevasse in a flying glissade. Now, however, nothing short of a glider would have been sufficient to perform such a feat, for the icy lips of the crevasse were fully fifty feet apart. I picked my way down a rocky point to the bottom and succeeded in scrambling over a low spot on the opposite wall.

The glacier crossed, I began to make my way over the loose moraine heaped up below it. A moraine, which gives way at every step, is more or less annoying to a climber both while going to or returning from an ascent, but particularly during the latter. This slope was so steep and the rocks imbedded in the clay so loosely that occasionally slides were precipitated as I carefully picked my way down.

As I swung around the lower end of the lake and walked up through a scattering of pines to camp, the roseate afterglow lighted up the rugged peaks by which the cirque is almost surrounded and touched with startling effect the rugged north face of Mt. Humphrey. The day's climbing had been adventurous for me. In fact, perhaps the dark angel hovered about at times and on one or two occasions may have come swooping down in my direction, but in the parlance of mountaineers, the climb was "interestingly difficult."

Up Mt. Thompson from the North
for the First Time

AROUND THE HEADWATERS of the South Fork of Bishop's Creek stand a number of high peaks well over 13,000 feet in elevation. Two of these, Mt. Thompson and Mt. Gilbert, are flat-topped, the former being the higher with an altitude of 13,480 feet. At the time which I have in mind, some thirty years ago, little climbing had been done in the area. In fact, some of the peaks had as yet not been ascended from the headwaters of the South Fork. Among these was Mt. Thompson. Precipitous, in places sheer, walls cut by occasional couloirs, some 1,500 feet in height, shoot up to its mesa-like summit. I had done some scanning of these with binoculars in search of a route and had found one or two possibilities.

Early one morning in the first week of September, I set out from Rainbow Camp, at an altitude of slightly over 9,000 feet, to attempt an ascent of the rather forbidding crags. From the end of the road, an elevation of some 10,000 feet, I struck out in a southwesterly direction, crossing a meadow at the upper end of South Lake. Above this I continued through a belt of broken, glaciated terrain, which soon brought me to the margin of a basin lying at timberline. Mt. Thompson was then within view, standing about a mile to the southwest. As the possible route which I had in mind ascended the mountain to the left of a prominent buttress projecting northeastward, I began to maneuver so as to approach it to best advantage.

Occupying cavities scooped out by glacial action, a chain of several lakes appeared. The first of these, as is usual with Sierra lakes, was remarkably clear, but the two upper ones, lying near the foot of a glacier, were tinged a beautiful turquoise by "rock flour" suspended in their waters. Having found a good vantage point from which to scan the precipitous face of Mt. Thompson, I sat down on a rock and began to do so. As not infrequently happens on rock walls rising above glaciers, the first several hundred feet appeared to be the most difficult portion of the climb. There seemed, however, to be a possibility of scaling the lower portion of the buttress for several hundred feet without encountering any special difficulty, but above that

86

there appeared to be a belt of about seventy-five feet which looked difficult to surmount. There appeared two possibilities of getting over it: one by clambering up a narrow crevice-like chimney; the other by scaling a wall to the right of it, apparently sufficiently broken to render it negotiable.

After continuing a short distance westward over glaciated rock, I swung to the southwest across a stretch of rough moraine and from the latter clambered up a rather steep pitch to the foot of the buttress. An escalade of about thirty feet up a sort of chute brought me to a wide ledge leading to the left. This I followed to the base of a narrow chimney. The wall to the right appeared to be scalable, so I decided to attempt it. Up its steep face I clambered for about fifty feet to a point at which it was necessary to traverse to the left. This would have to be accomplished by using a ledge which shelved downward at too steep an angle for safety, and there was a drop of several hundred feet immediately below it. I therefore thought it best to return and attempt the chimney.

This was evidently scalable but the angle was so steep, and insecurely lodged rocks so numerous, that its ascent would require extreme caution. In a preliminary maneuver my snow glasses fell from my pocket, and striking the rocks rather forcibly, were broken. The lower portion of the chimney proved to be a sort of back-and-knee method of progression. The walls were so close together that by jamming myself into the crevice I could work around most of the rocks without dislodging them as I slowly shoved myself upward. Within about twenty-five feet, however, I reached a point where I could clamber up with more freedom of movement. In view of a possible return by the same route, as I got above them I dislodged a considerable number of loose rocks, which after falling to the ledge below went ricocheting down the cliff below it. Within about fifty feet, I reached the head of the chimney and from it walked out onto a ledge. From my position the greater portion of the face appeared to be scalable, but what sort of climbing would be encountered below the summit remained to be seen.

Up the precipitous face of the mountain I rapidly picked my way, now following narrow ledges, now hoisting myself up over pitches intervening between them, gradually veering toward the crest of a rib leading toward the summit of the mountain. Eventually after some clambering up narrow chimneys and escalades over steep walls, I reached the broken crest. For several hundred feet I followed this, encountering rather aerial but not especially difficult climbing. To the left the arête fell away precipitously in couloirs with ribs between them; to the right, however, it fell away sheer to a large, snow-filled chute.

Eventually I came to a notch with a high pinnacle or gendarme standing beyond it. There appeared to be two possible alternatives in getting around this: one to descend a steep wall which appeared to have sufficient crevices to render it negotiable; the other to traverse the east face of the gendarme and scale the wall or chimney beyond it. Choosing the latter, I made my way down to the bottom of the notch from which I continued along ledges beyond it without encountering difficulty. The wall also appeared to be much less difficult than anticipated, a comparatively easy escalade of about a hundred feet bringing me to the rim of the mesa-like summit of the mountain.

The highest point of the summit was, however, about a half mile to the west. I therefore hastened across the top of the mountain, which declined somewhat to the left and gradually rose as I proceeded westward. Within a few hundred yards I came upon a narrow portion, where great couloirs had cut back so deeply into the mass of the mountain as almost to sever it. Beyond this I hurried onward to the foot of a pinnacle which I scaled, but seeing another apparently higher one about a hundred yards farther to the west, I descended from it and continued to the second. On the top of this I found a cairn, and in a glass jar placed in it about a half dozen names of climbers who had preceeded me.

As a heavy wind was blowing across the summit of the mountain, I did not tarry long. Luncheon and a superb view, detained me for a short while. Northward and northwestward I looked down into the spacious amphitheatre on the headwaters of Bishop Creek, its glaciated floor dotted with numerous lakes, and except to the northeast, surrounded by high mountains running well up over 13,000 feet, on the summit of one of which I sat. Conspicuous were the massive flat-topped Mt. Darwin to the northwest and the pyramidal form of Mt. Haeckel, a short distance to the south of it. Across the amphitheatre to the northwest the rugged form of Mt. Humphreys stood on the crest of the Sierra, along which the eye followed a long succession of high peaks to those of the Yosemite region, some fifty miles distant. In the opposite direction the view extended past the lofty Palisades only a few miles distant, southward to Mt. Whitney some sixty miles away. Immediately to the south I looked down a vertical mile to the Middle Fork of the Kings River.

Upon leaving the summit, I retraced my way to the point at which I had come over the rim. The northeastern face of the mountain was free from wind and I descended it rather leisurely. A number of rosy finches flitted from rock to rock ahead of me as I picked my way down the arête. Although the cirques were already filled with shadow, the upper portions of the mountains to the east and the southwest—notably the Palisades—were flooded with brilliant sunlight.

When I reached the narrow chimney, however, I encountered difficulties, due chiefly to loose rocks still lodged in it. After letting down my rucksack and ice axe I came upon a rock which it seemed best to dislodge. Before doing so, it was necessary to draw my *impedimenta* out of the way of the descending rock. While I was doing this my ice axe, insecurely attached, came loose and went clattering down the face of the mountain to its base.

After clearing out a few rocks preparatory to roping down, I looped my rope over a projecting rock, but upon inspecting it more closely, it appeared to be unsafe. I worked my way a short distance down to another, but distrusting this one also, I did not launch into space on a rappel, and used the rope merely as a support.

Eventually reaching the lower end of the chimney in safety, I traversed around the buttress on a ledge, and from the latter descended to the foot of the cliffs. After retrieving the ice axe, considerably the worse for the fall down the face of the mountain, I headed campward. The sun was now setting and a number of clouds which a heavy wind was driving over the summits of the mountains were suffused with roseate light.

I therefore hastened northward down glacially formed basins, and when I came to the last tier of cliffs, darkness was gathering fast. I continued downward over rough terrain to the meadow above South Lake, and from the latter climbed to the end of the road, where my car awaited me.

A Leisurely Ascent of Mt. Whitney by Trail

R ATHER EARLY ONE JUNE morning, I set out from Outpost Camp on Bighorn Flat—they sometimes call it Ibex Flat despite the fact that the ibex has never occurred in the Sierra, either in present or geologic times—at an altitude of some 10,500 feet on the Middle Fork of Lone Pine Creek. As I was not hankering for mountain climbing exploits, it would be a leisurely, one-foot-ahead-of-the-other procedure—the kind recommended by cautious persons and organizations.

On every side craggy granite mountains rose precipitously. After crossing the stream, fringed by a dense growth of alpine willow, the trail passes through an open grove of foxtail pines, abundant in this area in the Hudsonian Zone, and switchbacks up a moderately steep rise of several hundred feet, a step formed by a vanished glacier as it came cascading over somewhat resistant rocks that refused to be quarried out and carried down the canyon.

Above the rise the trail suddenly comes upon Mirror Lake, a rather small but very beautiful circular one hemmed in closely by granite mountains. Leaving the margin of Mirror Lake, the trail climbs up a rather steep slope through a grove of foxtail pines, the last sizeable trees to be seen on the way to the top of Mt. Whitney. Above the slope, the trail swings to a southwesterly direction following the crest of a glacially rounded hogback on which there is a scattering of dwarfed, contorted whitebark and foxtail pines, the vanguard of the trees that had struggled upward as far as severe climatic and other unforeseeable conditions had permitted them.

As I left the western end of the hogback, I rose above the upper margin of the Hudsonian and entered the Arctic-Alpine Zone, in which I would continue to be until I reached the top of Mt. Whitney.

The trail climbed steadily along a stream which came hurrying down the floor of a coulee-like canyon through a succession of small meadows. It was about the middle of July, and there was a profusion of bright-hued alpine flowers. In places the moist ground was yellow from thickly growing flowering mimulus. Lavender phacelia and pennyroyal clung to rocky slopes, while cyclamen with petals of the same hue but with golden centers grew abundantly in the small meadows. Luxuriant beds of *bryanthus* formed a carpet of rose-purple flowers on the ledges. The bases of the rocks were often fringed with the magenta flowers of the alpine epilobium, sometimes called rock fringe. Here and there ocean spray with a profusion of white flowers clambered up rocky pitches.

A short distance above timberline I passed a lake perhaps 200 yards in length, later named Consultation Lake. At an elevation of some 12,000 feet the trail entered a cirque lying immediately below the crest of the Sierra with Mt. Muir rising precipitously to an elevation of 14,025 feet beyond it. From the cirque the trail began to climb southward in long switchbacks toward the crest of a ridge more than 13,000 feet in elevation. Along it the delicate white and pink flowers of the Sierra primrose grew abundantly, apparently more so in this area than elsewhere in the Sierra. There were also the sunflower-like flowers of the hulsea, the blossoms an inch or so in diameter surmounting a stem with a maximum height of perhaps a foot. In this portion of the Sierra it persists to an altitude of more than 13,500 feet. Extremely abundant also were the vivid blue blossoms of the polemonium, which sometimes persists to an altitude of some 14,200 feet on the higher peaks, including Mt. Whitney.

In climbing Mt. Whitney by trail from the east, I usually abandon the latter in this cirque, and climb directly up a steep couloir, in the vicinity of Mt. Muir, to the crest of the Sierra, beyond which I intersect the trail. On this occasion, however, I followed the long, apparently interminable switchbacks toward the crest of the ridge, where it swings westward, and within a few hundred yards crosses that of the range at Whitney Pass, an altitude of 13,600 feet.

At the pass a magnificent view down into and across the great amphitheatre greets the climber of Mt. Whitney. Across it he rests his eyes on the Kaweahs, a stately group of peaks almost 14,000 feet in elevation, whose formation, in large part, harks back to a range preceding the present Sierra.

At the pass the trail drops several hundred feet on the west slope and then strikes out northward past Mt. Muir and continues along a line of spires, sometimes called Shark's Teeth, to the top of Mt. Whitney, a distance of slightly over two miles from the pass. By the time that I reached the latter, great cloud formations overshadowed the Sierra. To the north they hovered some distance above it in great, dark masses. Nowhere, however, did they envelop the crest of the range, and more than a hundred miles of it was visible. I could see from Mt. Langley, the most southerly of the 14,000-foot peaks of the Sierra, far north to the mountains of the Yosemite area. Eastward and southeastward the eye wanders over a vast expanse of alternating desert basins and arid ranges of mountains; to the west it looks down the gradually declining, forested west slope of the Sierra to the wide valley of the San Joaquin and beyond the latter to the even crestline of the Coast Range, blue in the distance. On the present occasion, a *chiaroscure* effect of deep shadow and bright sunlight overspread the vast panorama.

After surveying the latter for a few minutes, I sat down on a rock and began to eat luncheon. While I was doing so a brood of extremely tame rosy finches hopped to within several feet of me, picking up fragments of food which I tossed to them. The gentle and confiding disposition of these little birds, haunters of the summits of the Sierra, sometimes even in mid-winter, is very appealing.

While I sat eating luncheon, a snow squall passed over the summit of the mountain, but as it did not display any violent tendencies I paid little attention to it. Within a few minutes it was gone. After a sojourn of perhaps an hour on the summit, I headed southward back along the trail. Meanwhile the masses of clouds had begun to disperse and by the time that I reached Whitney Pass the sky was almost free of them. As I paused on the former, however, a mountain-like mass of clouds still hovered above the Kaweahs, some ten miles distant, beyond the great canyon of the Kern.

As I turned about, I noted that deep shadow was already creeping down from the summits on the crest of the Sierra. Eastward across the headwaters of the Middle Fork of Lone Pine Creek, the west slopes of Mts. Mallory, Irvine, and Lone Pine Peak were bright in the sunshine of late afternoon. But as I continued down the trail, deep shadow crept slowly up these, and when I reached camp the summits were glowing in the last roseate rays of the setting sun. Soon gray pallor overspread the granite mountains—the end of an extremely enjoyable day spent in a leisurely ascent of Mt. Whitney by trail.

First Ascent of the East Face of Mt. Whitney

 $\Large{A}$ MONG MOUNTAINEERS, SECOND in fascination to the making of first ascents is the finding of new routes up mountains already climbed, especially if these be difficult. As opportunities of accomplishing the former gradually diminish, climbers turn their attention to the discovery of new, more arduous ways of attaining the summits of mountains. Walking or riding being rather tame modes of reaching them in their estimation, they are forever seeking new problems of ascent against which they may match their skill and strength, puny as these may be compared with the forces of lofty mountains.

Scalable with comparative ease from south, west and north, Mt. Whitney, the highest peak in the United States proper, has lured mountaineers in quest of a "real climb." Last season a fairly difficult one was found leading from the east up a broad couloir culminating in a notch on an arête running northward from the peak and giving access to the north face, which was followed to the summit. Unsatisfied with this discovery, however, some climbers began to consider whether the apparently sheer east face of Mt. Whitney might not be scaled.

It was with this object in view that a party of five motored westward from Lone Pine toward the base of the Sierra Nevada during the forenoon of August 15, 1931. The group was one of proved climbing ability. It consisted of Dr. Robert Underhill of Harvard University, one of the most expert rock climbers in the United States; Francis Farquhar of San Francisco, prominent in the activities of the Sierra Club; Jules Eichorn from the same city, and Glen Dawson from Los Angeles, both youths, but very skillful in rock climbing; and the writer of this sketch.

Having arrived at the end of the road, some eight miles west of Lone Pine, we transferred our baggage from automobiles to the backs of several mules. After a short trudge up the sun-steeped eastern slope of the range, we swung around a shoulder and entered the refreshing coolness and shade of Lone Pine Canyon with the summit of Mt. Whitney looking down from its head a few miles directly to the west. Charmed by the alluring seclusions of the gorge with its floor shaded by pine and fir, with a brook resounding through a canopy of birch and willow, with

93

walls of mellow-hued and pleasingly-sculptured granite, we leisurely followed the trail to Hunter's Flat, a distance of about four miles, and continued up the switchbacks to the south of it to an elevation of some 9,000 feet above sea level. There the packs were removed from the mules.

After eating luncheon we fitted the packs to our own backs and, abandoning the trail, began to pick our way up the North Fork of Lone Pine Creek. Within a few hundred feet we came upon a projecting buttress around which we swung, and began to scramble over broken rocks in the direction of a crevice leading up a steeply shelving granite slope to a ledge running along the south wall of the gorge. Occasionally we stopped to regale ourselves in the luscious wild currants which grew abundantly among the chaotic talus through which we were passing. Below us the stream bounded along sonorously, hidden from view by a dense growth of birch and maple.

Upon arriving at the foot of the crevice, we scrambled up it as best we might, laden as we were with heavy and bulky packs, to the ledge which we followed around a projection. Although the ledge shelved down to a cliff, we strode rapidly along it in our rubber-soled shoes, pausing now and then to look down to the floor of the canyon several hundred feet below us, or turning about to gaze eastward through its V-shaped opening and across the wide basin of Owens Valley to the Inyo Mountains— richly colored, glowing in the afternoon sunshine and with a mass of snowy white cumulus clouds hovering above them. A scattering of limber pines grew along the lower portion of the shelf and as it gradually ascended, considerable numbers of foxtail pines began to appear. To our left a vertical wall of granite rose in places to a height of several hundred feet.

Having reached the upper end of the ledge, we crossed a strip of talus to the border of a glacially formed basin in which grew a beautiful grove of foxtail pines. Through these we filed along to the margin of a meadow at an altitude of some 10,000 feet. It was a fascinating spot, shut in to the north and south by craggy peaks and to the west by the great pinnacles and sheer walls of Mt. Whitney. Although it lies but a few miles from Owens Valley, this secluded recess has seldom seen human visitors since it is not on any trail and is difficult of access. Presently the sun sank behind the serrated peaks of Mt. Whitney, suffusing a few clouds that wreathed their summits with vivid-hued light.

The ensuing dawn was literally rosy-fingered, the peaks of Mt. Whitney and those on either side of the cirque glowing in roseate light of marvelous beauty. After a hasty breakfast, we were soon on our way northward across the meadow hoary with frost, to the base of a slope that we ascended to a cleft in the rock up which we scrambled to an apron-like slope of glaciated granite. Across this we picked our way along a series of cracks to a grove of foxtail pine in another basin. With this behind us, we clambered up to the point of a long promontory extending eastward from a shallow basin directly to the east of Mt. Whitney.

Along its narrow crest we sped nimbly to the margin of the upper basin where we halted for a few minutes in order to survey the face of Mt. Whitney, but being able to see very little of it, we walked northwestward a few hundred feet to a small lake which afforded a more satisfactory view. After careful scrutiny, a possible route was discovered. At best, however, it would be a difficult one and any of several apparent gaps in it might render it impracticable. After the first few hundred feet of comparatively easy climbing it led along narrow shelves, up steep chimneys and slabby faces to the left of a prow-like ridge dropping precipitously from the summit.

Our course decided upon, we left all unnecessary *impedimenta* including nailed shoes and an ice axe on a rock near the lake. In the matter of climbing equipment we took with us two alpine ropes averaging a 100 feet in length and a few pitons (spikes with iron rings through which to thread rope) for possible use in roping down. Our first objective was a notch between two gendarmes; along the face of one of these a ledge ran toward a couloir which we wished to ascend. The continuity of the shelf was problematic, however.

Up a steep acclivity, broken sufficiently to permit easy progress, we steadily climbed to the notch and there roped up. Dr. Underhill and Glen Dawson were on one rope; Jules Eichorn and myself were on the other. The first rope proceeded along the ledge but, as had been feared, it suddenly terminated in a sheer wall. Upon hearing this, the second rope began to scale the face of the gendarme, but this proved rather hazardous and we swung to the right and succeeded in finding a narrow shelf, or rather the edge of an upright rock slab with a crevice behind it, along which we made our way to a notch beyond the pinnacle. From this we descended a few feet, rounded a protruding buttress on narrow ledges, and began to ascend a chute, rather steep but with surface sufficiently roughened to afford good footing.

After an ascent of a few hundred feet we entered an alcove-like recess where further direct advance was barred by a perpendicular wall. There we awaited rope number one which presently arrived and after a short pause climbed over a low ridge into another couloir, rope number two following. Both ropes then clambered up an overhang to a platform. From this, however, progress upward could be made only by climbing a steep crack. Rather than run the risk of a fall, we decided to attempt a traverse around a buttress to the left, to a slabby couloir beyond it. As I swung out over the wall below the platform, an apparently firm rock gave way beneath my foot and went crashing down the sheer cliffs directly below, but as no one was in its path and my handholds were good, no harm resulted.

Rope number one then went around the buttress to reconnoiter and, after a pause, the other followed. The traverse proved to be one requiring considerable steadiness, as the ledges were narrow and there was a thousand feet of fresh air below. As we came around the projection we were confronted by a gap in a ledge with a narrow platform about eight feet below. There was the alternative of stepping across it—about the greatest distance a man of medium height could possibly reach, availing himself of rather poor handholds—or of dropping down to the platform and climbing the other side of the gap. Some members of the party chose one method, some chose the other. Once over the break in the ledge we were obliged to pull ourselves over a rounded rock by clinging to a diagonal crack with our hands while our feet swung out, momentarily, over the thousand-foot precipice. We then attacked a precipitous slabby wall, availing ourselves of narrow ledges for hand- and footholds. A few rods of this, however, brought us to a rounded shoulder with a broad couloir above it.

After halting a short time for luncheon we continued up the couloir zigzagging back and forth as we clambered over and around great granite steps until we were confronted at the upper end of the couloir by a vertical wall about thirty feet high. At one side of it, however, there was a narrow crevice up which one might scramble. After removing our rucksacks, we squirmed and "corkscrewed" up it, the last man tying the knapsacks to a rope carried by the first.

Above the couloir, somewhat to our surprise, we encountered rather easy climbing. We therefore unroped and began to ascend to the right toward the summit of Mt. Whitney. Within a few minutes we came within sight of the cairn, little more than two hundred feet above us. Quickening our speed, we clambered hastily upward, arriving at the summit considerably elated by the successful accomplishment of the first ascent of Mt. Whitney up its apparently unscalable eastern face. Francis Farquhar, having ascended the mountain by another route, was there to greet us.

The sky was almost cloudless and, due to recent storms, the atmosphere possessed a clarity unusual at that season of the year. Softly outlined against the southern horizon, far beyond the Sierra and across the Mojave Desert, we could descry the San Bernardino and San Gabriel Mountains; eastward the view extended far into Nevada, probably to the Charleston Mountains. Northward the eye followed a hundred miles of jagged peaks to the mountains of Yosemite. Westward across the upper basin of the Kern River, the stately Kaweahs and the dentated line of the Great Western Divide stood out with remarkable distinctness. A few white clouds hovered here and there in a deep blue sky. The air was almost motionless and the sunshine fell warm on the broad summit of the mountain.

After spending an hour or more on the top of Mt. Whitney, the party separated, three members following the trail southward in order to ascend Mt. Muir, while Dr. Underhill and I proceeded to descend the north face to a notch a few hundred feet below the summit. It was an easy descent along a rocky rib and down a wide couloir to the right of it. From the notch we obtained a superb view of Mt. Russell, with couloir-fluted face beyond a drop in the crest of the range. Turning abruptly at the notch, we began to go down a large chute which descends to the eastern base of Mt. Whitney. In it we came upon lingering remnants of polemonium, which a few weeks previously presented a gorgeous display of vivid blue flowers that scented the air with their delicious fragrance. Very few persons had ever traversed this couloir; with the exception of John Muir, probably none prior to 1930.

After emerging from the chute, we picked our way down a rocky slope to the lake at which we had cached some of our superfluous articles. The placid lake still gleamed in the sunshine, although the shadows of the mountains were slowly creeping across the basin. Having gathered up the *impedimenta* we went southward to the brow of a cliff which we descended to a moraine-strewn depression. While skirting the base of the former, our attention was attracted to a profusion of rose epilobium —sometimes appropriately called rock fringe on account of its habit of growing along the margin of rocks. Its rose-purple flowers are among the most beautiful of the high Sierra, and they often persist well into autumn.

Within a half mile we passed a deep blue lake to our right and after swinging to the left, walked along another, nestling at the entrance to a cirque. Presently we were traveling through a grove of foxtail pines with rich red-brown boles and storm-rent boughs, perhaps the most picturesque of Sierra conifers. Continuing down the glaciated granite, we observed clusters of red flowering wild fuchsia in a setting of sober gray rocks. Then within a few minutes we were at the base of the cliffs and in a few more minutes, in camp. Some two hours later the other members of the party returned from their ascent of Mt. Muir.

After an evening spent consuming enormous quantities of food and lounging about the campfire, we retired to our sleeping bags under nearby foxtail pines, solemn and silent beneath a sky spangled with countless stars overarching the mountains that loomed darkly around the basin. On the following morning we made up our packs and proceeded down the canyon, pleased at having added another outstanding climb to the many already discovered in the Sierra Nevada.

Up Mt. Whitney from the North

M Y CAMP WAS IN AN open grove of foxtail pines at an altitude of some 10,000 feet above the sea on the North Fork of Lone Pine Creek. Eastward I looked down the deep, rugged gorge of the latter and across the wide floor of Owens Valley to the pleasingly-blended colorings of the Inyo Range. Much of it is composed of metamorphic formations, harking back to Paleozoic times, laid down beneath a sea that then extended across the present site of the Sierra and far eastward.

On the preceding day I had come up the canyon, carrying a rather heavy pack. As the floor of the former is covered by a dense growth of willow, birch, chinquapin, and other small trees and shrubs, I avoided it by following a wide ledge running along the face of the south wall of the canyon, until it eventually terminated a short distance below the flat upon which I had made camp.

This flat lay along the lower margin of a cirque, westward across which the precipitous east face of Mt. Whitney rose to its summit, an elevation of 14,495 feet. Somewhat weary of climbing Mt. Whitney by trail, I had, on previous occasions, rather toilsomely made my way up the canyon of the North Fork, and ascended by a large couloir which terminates on the crest of the range immediately north of Mt. Whitney's summit. My plans on this occasion were rather vague, but I eventually decided to cross the col or saddle immediately north of Mt. Whitney and attempt the ascent of the latter by its steep, couloir-fluted north face.

Early on the following morning, therefore, I left camp, carrying only rucksack, rope and ice axe. A deep blue sky overarched the lofty mountains that hemmed in the cirque on the headwaters of the stream. Although it was mid-July, the air was cold and crisp.

After clambering up over a few hundred feet of talus blocks, I scaled a tongue of rock running eastward from a shallow basin lying immediately below the precipitous east face of the mountain. My route lay along ledges, up over short vertical pitches, and eventually along the crest of an arête which I followed for several hundred yards to the margin of the basin. This lies at an altitude of some 12,000 feet, covered with disintegrated granite strewn with a scattering of frost-shattered rocks, and might be 200 yards in width. In the middle there is a shallow lake.

As I sat down on a rock along the margin of the lake, I noticed a number of rosy finches busily feeding on dead and benumbed insects strewn about on the granite sand, perhaps carried upward and deposited there by strong rising currents of air, which not infrequently occurs in the Sierra. When it does, the rosy finches seem in some way to become aware of it and lose no time in reaching the place to feast upon the insects.

From the lake I looked southwestward up the apparently sheer east face of Mt. Whitney. To the northwest rose the couloir-furrowed north face of Mt. Russell, 14,190 feet in elevation. Between the two mountains lies a col perhaps 12,500 feet in elevation. My plan was to cross this col on the crest of the range and ascend the north face of Mt. Whitney. This did not appear to be inordinately difficult and as I had previously scanned it, seemed to promise interesting climbing. As yet perhaps Mt. Whitney had not been ascended up this entire face, but I was not entirely certain that such was the case because John Muir may have traversed it on his descent from the mountain.

As I was picking my way up the slope, a pair of rock wrens chattered as they darted in and out among the rocks in quest of lurking insects, at times coming within a few feet of me. These plucky little birds sometimes occur at an elevation of 14,000 feet in the Sierra. The slope was dotted with the vivid blue, mound-like clusters of polemonium, and the air was pervaded by their spicy, almost musky fragrance.

I reached the pass without encountering any difficulties and then swung to the left and began to diagonal southward toward the north face of Mt. Whitney, picking my way along shelves on the face of a ridge. Here and there I came upon a patch of steeply slanting hard-frozen snow which necessitated the cutting of a few steps.

Upon reaching the base of Mt. Whitney I paused and carefully surveyed the couloir-furrowed north face rising above me. As the portion immediately to the right of the ridge appeared to be too sheer to afford safe climbing, I continued several hundred yards farther to a more broken area. There, after cutting steps across a slope of hard-frozen snow, I began to force my way up a rather precipitous chute. For some distance the occurrence of quantities of glare ice obliged me to do some careful step cutting. Eventually I reached the head of the couloir. Above this an area of steeply tilted slabby rock required cautious maneuvering in order to avoid a possible slip, which might result in my plunging over a tier of cliffs immediately below.

After traversing several hundred feet of this rather treacherous terrain, however, I came to a rib which appeared to offer a feasible route to the summit of the mountain, then about 800 feet above me. This afforded interesting rock work, as I clambered up it, now along its crest, now along ledges on one or the other side of it. On my way I enjoyed numerous striking views of the south face of Mt. Russell, rising steeply immediately across a narrow cirque to the north. Seen from this direction, it is a superbly beautiful mountain.

A half hour or so of steady climbing then brought me to, the foot of a parapet-like wall. I hoisted myself up over this only to discover that I was standing on the rim of the broad and gently sloping summit of Mt. Whitney. Picking my way across its surface strewn with plaque-like slabs of granite wrenched by frost from the underlying rock, I headed toward the highest point of the mountain, an elevation of 14,495 feet.

The sky was cloudless and the atmosphere so clear that the entire range stood out with remarkable distinctness. After surveying the immense panorama for a few minutes I sat down on a sun-baked rock and removed my luncheon from my rucksack. Several rosy finches hopped up to within a few feet of me picking up fragments of food scattered about on the surface of the rocks. Their cheery, confiding disposition, their somewhat musical calls, and their attractive coloring—a pleasing blending of gray and black set off by a wash of rose purple on the upper portions of their body—render these gentle birds the favorites of Sierra mountaineers.

In the warm sunshine a feeling of lethargy crept over me. In about two hours, however, I shook it off and picking up my rucksack, rope and ice axe, walked over to the rim of the north face of the mountain. Down this, a somewhat precipitous face of alternating avalanche-formed chutes and sharp, intervening ribs, I picked my way for perhaps 500 feet.

There I came to a rather conspicuous notch in the crest of

101

the ridge running northward from Mt. Whitney. Passing through this I came to the head of a very large couloir running down the east face of the mountain. Down this I continued for several hundred feet and then abandoned it in favor of ledges running along its precipitous south wall. Both on the floor of the chute and on the ledges of its walls grew great numbers of polemonium, larger than any I had seen elsewhere. Here untold generations of them had flourished but no human being except John Muir and myself had ever enjoyed their beauty.

After descending a few hundred feet, I swung to the right out of the couloir to the face of the mountain which was there sufficiently broken to afford only moderately difficult climbing. Soon I reached the shallow basin lying at its base. Hearing a report like that of a rifle, I turned around to ascertain its cause. A large block of granite wrenched loose from the crags had fallen into the large couloir which I had descended an hour or so previously. So great was its velocity that it ricocheted several hundred feet before striking the floor of the chute a second time. It was one of a myriad of rocks that had come crashing down in the formation of the couloir.

I passed the shallow lake to the farther side of the basin and from there continued along the arête extending eastward from it. By this time the shadows of the lofty peaks on the crest of the Sierra were creeping across the cirques below them. Eastward across the wide floor of Owens Valley, still more than a vertical mile below, the sunshine of late afternoon fell bright on the soft but rich colors of the Inyo Mountains.

Reaching the termination of the arête, I swung to the right down over a succession of ledges. In the basin in the same direction, a few hundred feet below me lay a deep lake of ultramarine blue. As I reached the foot of the tier of cliffs and continued downward over the granite blocks of a talus slope, I observed a considerable number of fragile columbines tinted delicate yellow and deep orange, waving airily among the blocks of granite.

Eventually skirting a small lake and passing through a thicket of alpine willows I reached my camp. My day had been very interesting; John Muir is probably the only other person besides myself to have gone exploring in the terrain on the north face of Mt. Whitney, and the great couloir to the east.

Solo Afoot Across the Sierra Nevada in Autumn

L EAVING CEDAR GROVE AT the lower end of the Grand Canyon of the South Fork of the Kings River on the morning of September 22, I trudged up the gently inclining floor of the canyon for a few miles and made camp under a great ponderosa pine on a point overlooking the river and commanding a superb view up the canyon. Groves of cotton-woods bordering the river and deciduous oak on the slope immediately south of my camp were already showing evidence of the approach of autumn in splashes of yellow and orange foliage.

For a number of years I had been in the habit of occasionally visiting the canyon, but usually merely passed through it on my way to and from the high mountains, or if, perchance, I remained a few days, it was generally an interruption of a long and arduous trip along the crest of the Sierra, during which I did little in the way of exploring the canyon floor. On this occasion, however, I contemplated spending upwards of a week rambling about in the canyon, particularly on the south side of the river, with which, despite my frequent visits, I had little acquaintance.

The floor of the canyon is open in places but most often it is clothed with a stand of ponderosa and sugar pines and a sprinkling of incense cedar. Occasionally there are thickets of the latter on the moist bottoms along the river which is frequently bordered by a line of cottonwoods and alders. Rocky slopes sweeping up to the foot of the crags often display groves of deciduous oak, while the golden-cup oak, an evergreen variety, clings to the crags themselves whenever it can find footing.

After spending several delightful days wandering about on the floor of the canyon, enjoying almost numberless beautiful vistas up and down the emerald current of the tree-shaded river, I packed up, and proceeding several miles farther eastward, made camp along Copper Creek. This clear, cold stream flows into the South Fork not far from the head of the Grand Canyon. It is overhung by alders and bordered to the west by a strip of rather dense incense cedars. Beyond these stretch open stands of

103

ponderosa and sugar pines. Among them during my sojourn of a few days I saw bands of deer and once or twice a bear went lumbering through them.

The floor of the canyon is here about 5,000 feet in elevation. Directly opposite my camp and only about a quarter of a mile distant, the Grand Sentinel rises in great crags of various-hued gray granite tinged in places by vivid nuances of green, to an altitude of 8,514 feet. The play of deep shadow and bright sunlight across its rugged front was very impressive both morning and evening.

On the first day of October, despite my having eaten an almost unbelievable number of them during the summer in my solitary ramblings, I felt that I would relish a mess of trout. Taking my fly casting outfit, I walked to the upper end of the Grand Canyon, perhaps a mile and a half distant, and then continued up the stream as it comes leaping down a deep canyon from the northeast. After continuing with a gentle angle for perhaps a half mile, the floor of the canyon veers and rises at a steep angle to Paradise Valley, some four miles distant, down which the stream flows in almost continuous cascades. Here lie great numbers of pools in which rainbow trout of moderate size abound. Working from pool to pool, often over and around great blocks of granite which had rolled down from high cliffs on either side of the stream, I spent a fascinating day in the warm, mellow and bright sunshine of Sierra October. I only spent a part of it fishing, however, since the limit in the Kings Canyon is fifteen. After catching this number I rambled about enjoying the magnificent rugged canyon scenery. The trout caught were all rainbows, most of them pan-sized, but several were about a foot in length.

Several days later I packed up and continued eastward to the head of the Grand Canyon and thence up the trail as it climbs steeply up the canyon of Bubbs Creek. Near the mouth of Sphinx Creek, at an elevation of 6,500 feet, I made camp in a grove of tall pines and cedars. Nearby the stream raced along beneath bordering cottonwoods. Through the green foliage I caught glimpses of thickets of deciduous oaks, the leaves of which were fast changing to yellow, orange and russet, adorning the talus slope running up to the base of granite crags.

A short distance below my camp Bubbs Creek plunges down a deep gorge. The narrow floor of this gorge is strewn with great boulders around which the stream goes leaping in continuous cascades, varied by numerous deep pools in which rainbow trout are abundant. On the following day, wishing another mess of trout, I assembled my fishing equipment and descended to the head of the gorge.

The stream had obviously been fished considerably during the summer, at least in the more accessible pools. Others more difficult of approach, especially those which required a somewhat difficult cast, appeared to harbor plenty of trout. In one in midstream I caught a good-sized rainbow. I was obliged to hang down over the vertical face of a rock several feet high, in some danger of an unwished-for headlong plunge into the eddying pool, to slip my net beneath the exhausted fish. Luckily, however, I was able to retrieve it without mishap. In another case— a rather long cast across a waterfall and into a pool overhung by alder boughs on the farther side of the stream—twelve or fifteen casts netted me a half-dozen pan-sized rainbows. Enough trout for supper and breakfast, together with the enjoyment of the wildly rugged scenery—the river cascading down beneath overhanging alders, lofty sugar and ponderosa pines and incense cedars, above these golden-cup oaks clinging to granite crags rising precipitously for several thousand feet.

The next day I continued up the trail leading toward the headwaters of the stream. As I trudged along I passed through numerous groves of pine and increased numbers of fir. In places there were groves of cottonwood trees, the foliage of which, as the altitude increased, displayed more and more vivid yellow. At times the trail wound along through beds of ferns waist— occasionally almost shoulder—high, the fronds of which were already changing to a soft lemon hue.

About the middle of the afternoon, at an elevation of perhaps 7,500 feet, I came to a grove of ponderosa pines on a west-facing slope. The sunshine fell with mellow warmth and brightness in the open stand of pines and the stream flowed past within a few yards. It was indeed a deligthful place to camp. Throwing down my pack, I removed my Hudson Bay cruiser axe from the packboard to which it was lashed and proceeding to a scattering of deciduous oaks a short distance above, chopped down a long dead one some eight inches in diameter, from which I cut two lengths of several feet. These placed parallel a few inches apart on a space made level with my axe made an excellent "woodsman's range." With my ice axe I then raked together the long dry needles of the pines to a bed a foot or more in depth on the down-canyon side of a great block of granite in order to afford shelter from the night wind.

This done, I removed my fly rod from the case lashed to the packboard on the side opposite to the axe, and getting together my tackle, went down to the margin of the stream. For several minutes I received no response and then in a rather large pool across a bit of swift water I hooked, played and eventually landed a Loch Leven slightly under fourteen inches in length. I was soon hooking and landing both Loch Leven and rainbow trout, the former often near the outlet of pools, the latter more frequently under waterfalls or in short stretches of fast, broken water.

The fishing was decidedly autumn in tone. The stream was far below its summer level. It was overhung in places by the deep red of the berries of the mountain ash. On the steep banks of the trench down which it flowed, the foliage of wild cherry, thimbleberry, mountain maple, and other shrubbery was fast changing to yellow. Here and there a clump of birches along the margin of the stream was already yellow, orange and crimson, glowing in the sunshine of late afternoon. A short distance above my camp stood the first grove of aspen trees which I had observed. Their foliage was in part still summer green, but in part already lemon yellow, brilliant orange and deep carmine. For several days I remained at this fascinating spot, each day catching without difficulty all the trout that I needed—but no more— from the stream.

Taking up my pack again I continued toward the crest of the Sierra. I had not gone far when the groves of cottonwoods and aspen had almost reached their maximum of autumn coloring. Toward evening, at an elevation of 8,500 feet, I came to a widening of the floor of the canyon, clothed in considerable part by groves of cottonwood and aspen all of gorgeous autumn hues. Northward the face of granite crags was carved into great rounded buttresses, southward steep gray granite slopes, clad in places with clumps of dark firs, swept up toward high peaks. The spot was too wildly beautiful to pass. Therefore I made camp in a clump of brilliant aspens not far from the stream.

Taking my fly casting equipment on the following morning, I went upstream. Above the flat on which I was camped at the mouth of East Creek, Bubbs Creek comes leaping down over a rather long stretch of steep, shelving glaciated granite. To the casual observer such an incline would not seem likely to contain any pools suitable for harboring trout. Echeloned along it, as it were, there are numerous deep bowl-like basins in which lurk numerous trout, both Loch Leven and rainbow. In the first pool, my luck was varied. After losing a trout or two by carelessly maneuvering them across a bit of swift water at the outlet of the pool, I hooked and landed several medium-sized fish.

For a while thereafter, my coordination, as I suppose happens at times to all trout fishermen, was somewhat at fault. Through inaccurate or faulty timing I seemed almost alternately to hook or miss good strikes. Possibly too I was paying as much or more attention to the scenery than to the manipulation of my rod and line, as the view obtained in every direction was impressive. Here and there clumps of birch, their yellow, orange and red foliage suffused with brilliant sunlight, arched the banks of the stream along which there were fringes of dogwood, the leaves of which were now a deep crimson, while up over rough talus slopes thickets of young aspen trees, their foliage glowing yellow and carmine, trembled in fitful gusts of breeze and flashed in the autumn sunshine.

After going above the brow of the steep incline, I continued to fish along a succession of pools, some of them very large. Casting over a rock into a rather small one, I hooked a trout, and to my surprise discovered that it was large. The smallness of the pool, an undercut rock on one side and swift water above and below it, rendered the playing of the fish somewhat difficult. Eventually however I succeeded in maneuvering it in an exhausted condition up to the bank and, slipping my net under it, lifted it from the pool. It proved to be a Loch Leven at least eighteen inches in length, an unusually large fish for a Sierra stream so small as Bubbs Creek at this elevation.

With all the trout that I needed I returned down the trail to camp. I discovered that two fishermen had crossed the crest of the Sierra from the east, and continuing down the west slope, had camped the preceding evening a short distance above me. During the day each had caught the limit of rainbows. At their camp in a clump of tall fir trees, we had a combined trout feed. The big Loch Leven, however, was reserved to grace an urban trout feast on the return of the two fishermen to their homes in Los Angeles.

During that evening the Indian summer weather seemed to be ending. From the southwest came masses of clouds threatening a storm. I had contemplated remaining several days longer, but one can never be certain that an October storm may not deposit several feet of snow along the crest of the southern Sierra Nevada, so I decided to cross the crest the next day with the fishermen whom I had met.

Starting out rather early, we began the long ascent to Kearsarge Pass which, although the lowest one for many miles along this portion of the crest of the Sierra, is 11,823 feet above the sea. At Bullfrog Lake, an elevation of some 10,500 feet we halted for luncheon. Masses of heavy clouds hung over the high peaks, and a cold wind swept across the lake. On our way again, we trudged up to the pass, and then went rapidly along the trail leading down the steep eastern escarpment of the Sierra. At an elevation of some 8,500 feet, we came to the end of the road at which my companions had parked their car. In a few minutes we were speeding down the road and within a half hour were on the floor of Owens Valley. Thus terminated another of my numerous trips afoot across the Sierra.

Three Weeks in Autumn on the Middle Fork of the Kings River: The Sierra Nevada

"I SHALL HAVE THE MOUNTAINS all to myself," I reflected as I observed a trail crew, the last party to come out from the Middle Fork of the Kings River, descending from Bishop Pass, 12,000 feet above the sea on the main crest of the southern Sierra Nevada. It was October 14 and fearing they might be cut off from crossing to the east side by snow on the pass, several feet of which might fall at any time, they were leaving the mountains even though their work was unfinished. As I crossed the pass, the light of the setting sun brightened and eventually became roseate on the summit of Mt. Agassiz, a fine peak 13,891 in elevation rising a short distance to the east. The sunlight soon failed, but presently the moon, now almost full, emerged from behind the North Palisade, a superb peak over 14,000 feet, two miles to the southeast. High peaks in every direction were flooded with the bright but mellow light.

After following the trail for perhaps two miles beyond the pass, I halted and threw down my pack in a clump of lodgepole and whitebark pines at an elevation of 10,500 feet. I camped at this particular spot because two months previously I had boxed up a considerable amount of food and cached it underneath nearby rocks. Finding the food undisturbed, I packed it up and next morning descended the trail leading to the Middle Fork of the Kings River. My pack was rather heavy, weighing perhaps a hundred pounds, but as I expected to spend several weeks without any opportunity of replenishing my food supply other than by fishing, I preferred to take along an ample amount.

Early in the afternoon I reached the floor of the canyon, there an elevation of some 8,500 feet. After depositing my pack in a grove of pines and firs along the margin of the river, I got out my fly fishing outfit. "I may as well have a mess of golden trout for supper," I thought.

The preceding winter had seen unusually light snowfall, and the summer had been almost rainless, so the river was exceptionally low—the lowest, in fact, for a number of years. The melting snow from the high basins had almost ceased and autumn rains had not yet arrived. Using a queen of waters and a flight's fancy, I began to cast from a portion of the dry, gravelly bed of the stream. I wondered how the trout would respond to my flies; they do not always take them with avidity so late in the season in the Sierra Nevada.

I had not long to wait, however, for within a half dozen casts, an eight-inch golden trout, darting from underneath a rock, struck the queen of waters vigorously, and after a bit of playing about in the stream, its brilliant golden hues lay on the gravelly beach. A short distance above I entered the lower end of a small gorge, down which the river cascaded, leaping from pool to pool. Here I caught sufficient pan-sized trout for supper and breakfast. Satisfied with my catch, I returned to my pack and set about making camp.

On the following day—a beautiful one of bright, mellow sunshine—I went upstream, beginning to fish a short distance above the head of the small gorge. After fishing a stretch of pools, I traversed a meadow, and began to cast again in the deep pools made by the stream in another small gorge—a much more thrilling form of trout fishing than whipping the quiet stretches of river in the meadow below. Leaping from rocks to the sound of cascading water, I cast my flies down and across the stream, for the most part into deep pools, some lying a lucid emerald in bright sunshine, others dark from being shaded by overhanging rocks. Although the trout taken were usually pan-sized, now and then I caught one upwards of a foot in length. They were not especially wary, but all, particularly the larger ones, appreciated a well-placed fly, sometimes making several darts toward one, but not actually striking until it alighted in the proper spot and in an approved fashion.

At the foot of a falls of considerable height I halted, and having removed the trout from my creel, was somewhat surprised to find that I had already caught the limit of twenty. As a rule, when traveling alone in the mountains, I prefer to catch a maximum of about a dozen pan-sized trout—fewer, of course, if larger—in other words, enough for two or at most three meals. By observing this precaution, my trout are always fresh, and I am never surfeited with fish or fishing, not to mention unnecessarily depleting the number of trout by taking more than can be used. The next day, therefore, I would be obliged to refrain from fishing.

On the following morning I packed up and began to descend the trail down the river. On either side of the canyon, es-

110

pecially to the west, granite walls, in many places sheer, rise for upwards of 2,000 feet, and above and beyond jutting promontories one catches glimpses of high peaks. It is a marvelously beautiful stretch of canyon. After traveling a few miles I halted and made camp on Palisade Creek, a stream entering the Middle Fork from the east at an elevation of some 8,000 feet.

Early the next morning I set out to catch a mess of golden trout in Palisade Creek. Again I caught the limit, but with my voracious mountain appetite, I had no difficulty in disposing of them in three meals. They would also, in all probability, be my last golden trout, for below the mouth of Palisade Creek the golden are soon succeeded by the rainbow, 8,000 feet usually being the altitude at which golden trout are found in southern Sierra streams.

Immediately below the mouth of Palisade Creek the walls of the canyon on either side converge so as to form a deep narrow gorge six or eight miles in length. Down the narrow floor the river cascades, dropping a thousand feet in that distance. Following a rough trail the next day, I descended to the mouth of Cartridge Creek. There I was in a different climate. Ponderosa and sugar pines, together with incense cedar, were common. Cottonwoods and alders bordered the stream. Evergreen oaks clung to the bluffs, while some of the gentler slopes were covered with deciduous ones. Summer, too, still lingered here, for a great portion of the foliage of the alder and the cottonwood remained unchanged.

In a clump of ponderosa pines and incense cedars I made my camp. In the morning I got out my fly casting outfit and went down to Cartridge Creek. The casting was excellent. The stream was fairly wide, and, although bordered in many places by alders and cottonwoods, these did not interfere appreciably with the manipulation of a good length of line. When they did, the water was so low, compared with that of summer, that even in midstream one could leap from one boulder to another. Unfortunately these boulders, washed down by high water, and usually resting on a gravelly bottom, were not always very stable. On more than one occasion they rolled under the impact of my weight, precipitating me into the stream. The volume and depth of the water, however, was so low that this never resulted in more than a good wetting.

111

The trout struck about as vigorously as they do in summer. Isolated by 12,000 foot passes to the east, north and south and by a thirty mile trek through the forest to the northwest, this portion of the canyon of the Middle Fork of the Kings River is visited by comparatively few fishermen. Not only is the rainbow trout fishing extremely good, but the canyon is one of the most delightfully sequestered places in the Sierra Nevada. One has a feeling, especially when it has been deserted by summer travellers, of being very remote from the homes and haunts of men.

On the following day I went fishing again and could not refrain from catching twenty-five. However, the trout with a few exceptions were pan-sized averaging some eight inches in length, and I had developed an inordinate capacity for consuming trout, partly, perhaps, because of my being entirely without fresh meat. Being in a national park, I could, of course, shoot nothing. I kept the trout in a cool spring a few rods from my camp, so there was no danger of any being wasted.

I lingered another day in my camp beneath the great ponderosa pines, enjoying to the full the autumn weather, and to me, the delightfully sequestered canyon. Next morning, however, I broke camp, and descended the gradually sloping floor of the canyon a few miles to Simpson Meadow lying at an elevation of 6,000 feet. The Middle Fork of the Kings, from Simpson Meadow to the Tehipite Valley, a distance of some twelve miles, is strikingly beautiful. The stream flows rapidly with smooth, deep current, and breaks into stretches of foaming rapids or cascades, forming an apparently numberless succession of deep emerald pools. It is bordered in many places by lines of cottonwood and alder, and lofty ponderosa and sugar pines together with incense cedar clothe the slopes on either side. As one descends the river, deciduous oak becomes more abundant. On either side of the floor of the canyon precipitous, in many places sheer, walls of granite rise for several thousand feet.

My day on the stream was full of minor accidents, due—as is usually the case—to negligence. Having snagged my flies more than once in overhanging alder boughs by careless casting, I was obliged to indulge in some arboreal gymnastics to retrieve them. Once I waded the river waist deep to recover a fly swept under the water and fastened on a submerged log. The prize bit of negligence, however, was my leaping onto a water-washed boulder in mid-stream. Even the crepe soled canvas shoes which I was wearing would not hold on this. Sliding from the marble smooth surface my hip collided with the rock in anything but gentle fashion, and the rod broke its tip. Fortunately I had a duplicate and it was only a matter of a few minutes time out to replace the broken rod.

With a fine mess of trout in my creel, I threaded my way underneath the great pines, as the sun was about to dip behind the walls of the canyon. The hours of fishing along the conifer-shaded stream had been among the most pleasant that I had enjoyed during the entire trip. But the beautiful weather could not continue indefinitely. For several days there had been some indications of an approaching change. That evening the sky became obscured by heavy clouds. By nine o'clock rain was falling. It continued during the entire night, and, with some intermissions, throughout the following day. On the succeeding night it rained for a while and then began to snow.

When I awoke the trees were heavily burdened with the snow and about six inches of it lay on the ground. "Tehipite Valley for me today!" I exclaimed as I crawled out of my sleeping bag and stirred up the fire. Breakfast over, I crossed the river, which had risen considerably during the night, and followed the trail leading down the canyon. From time to time masses of wet snow falling from the trees struck me as I passed underneath them. I had hoped to enjoy the view of the fine granite walls which rise above this twelve-mile stretch of canyon, but they were completely shrouded in dense vapor.

Late in the afternoon I reached the upper end of Tehipite Valley. I had not been here for years, so my return was especially pleasing. It is one of the finest "Yosemites," as John Muir would term it. Its outstanding feature is the Tehipite Dome which vies with the Half Dome of the Yosemite Valley. Not so massively grand as the latter, it is perhaps more beautifully symmetrical, as it springs from the floor of the canyon for some 3,500 feet, much of it sheer granite, gradually tapering to a comparatively small dome.

On the floor of the valley, slightly over 4,000 feet, the vegetation differs considerably from that of Simpson Meadow. On the lower slopes and along the talus at the foot of the crags the golden-cup oak is the predominant tree. On the less rocky slopes the deciduous oak is abundant. The river is lined by cottonwoods, alders, laurels, and large-leafed maples. The ponderosa pine and the incense cedar are common, and the last of the sugar pines are some distance upstream.

I followed the vestige of a trail a mile and a half downstream to the Little Tehipite. At the lower end of the valley, not only the topography but the rocks change with startling abruptness. The great glacier, or perhaps a succession of them, that once came down the canyon from the crest of the Sierra, reached their farthest limit at the lower end of the Tehipite Valley. The U-shaped cross section of the upper portion of the canyon therefore ceases at that point and is succeeded by a V-shaped gorge which continues for some thirteen miles to its junction with that of the South Fork. The walls along this lower stretch of canyon are extremely high. Along a portion of it there is a vertical difference of 8,000 feet between the floor of the canyon and the summit of Spanish Mountain immediately to the north. Along the lower end of the Tehipite runs a contact fault or break in the rocks. Above this is the pure granite of which the batholith or heart of the Sierra is formed; below it is a confused mass of dark metamorphic rocks, altered greatly from the original igneous and sedimentary rocks by heat and pressure.

After an hour spent in reconnoitering in the vicinity, I went down to the river to try the fishing. So high were the walls of the canyon that, although it was mid-forenoon, the sun had not yet appeared above the rim. On account of the coldness of the air, flying insects were not yet active. When the sun appeared and the insects began to stir, the trout struck at my flies. At noon, with a dozen fine rainbows, I lounged about a while in the pleasing mellow brightness and mild warmth of a day in the last week of October.

Seldom have I had a more pleasant time in the mountains than the week which I spent there. The weather was delightful. The foliage of the alder trees was still a midsummer green. The deciduous oaks were orange and green. The leaves of the cottonwood were evenly divided between summer green and autumn yellow. Underneath the oaks and in the thicket of manzanita were numerous coveys of the beautiful mountain quail. The California grey squirrel lithely leaped from bough to bough in pine and oak, or bounded along the ground. Now and then I came upon a band of deer, both those which had been there during the summer, and others, which the recent storm had driven from the higher mountains.

114

Within a week, however, a wind from the southwest brought up heavy masses of clouds. Another storm was obviously approaching. To attempt to return over the crest of the Sierra without snowshoes was out of the question, since the last storm had probably deposited several feet of snow there. If I lingered much longer I might find even the 8,000 foot pass, the lowest available to the northwest, also blocked with snow. It was already storming when I left the Tehipite. Up a steep, zigzag trail I trudged some 3,000 feet to the rim of the canyon.

I spent the night in a cabin left unlocked at Crown Valley. During the night the temperature continued to fall until in early morning it was at least zero. I was soon on my way, following the trail as it ran westward through the magnificent stand of conifers which still clothes a great portion of the west slope of the Sierra Nevada. As I approached the pass the snow gradually became deeper until it reached my knees. I do a considerable amount of winter traveling in the Sierra, but as a rule on skis. Wading through miles of snow without even anything in the way of makeshift snowshoes has no great appeal to me.

The snow had obliterated the trail, and the blazes on the trees were infrequent and so old as to be almost unrecognizable. Eventually I lost the trail, but keeping its general direction, wading through the snow, at last I reached the floor of the valley.

Because this was considerably lower, the snow decreased in depth. On the trail were fresh horse tracks made (as I learned later) by stockmen traveling into the mountains to pick up strays. Being unfamiliar with the country, and having almost walked off my maps, I thought it best to follow the horse tracks until I should reach the camp of the party and procure definite information about the region.

I remained overnight with the two riders at their camp and on the following morning went down with them several miles southward. They pointed out a cow trail leading south and within several miles intersecting the one which I wished to follow westward. I followed it across a wide valley clothed with a stand of superb ponderosa and sugar pines. The trail, however, grew dimmer as I advanced, and it was crossed by so many other cow trails that it became difficult to follow. Eventually— so it seemed—it dwindled to a squirrel track that ran up a pine tree and into hole. I was not particularly concerned because the forest was so open that it was as easy to travel through it without a trail as with one, and I knew that within a mile or so I would intersect the one which I sought.

I found it running westward along the crest of a rounded ridge. The ridge eventually narrowed, and from it I looked far down into the profound canyon of the Kings River, some distance below the mouth of the Middle Fork. Knowing that I was leaving the high mountains, I threw down my pack and climbed to the summit of a rock to look eastward. From it I gazed far up the South Fork of the Kings River to the crest of the Sierra which was already white with snow. Picking up my pack again, I strode along for a few miles more through stands of magnificent pines. Toward evening I halted at a small spring and made camp. It was to be my last one in the conifer forest.

On the following morning I felt like lingering for a day, but it was already November 4. Within a few miles the trail left the pines and followed the ridge, now open, rapidly downward. Bands of deer bounded away as I passed along the trail. I was soon in the upper foothills with their groves of oaks. The grass was already becoming green from the first autumn rains. The country was beautiful in its way, but having left behind the high Sierra and the great belt of conifer forest on its west slope, somehow it had little attraction for me. That evening I came to a road and in the morning I secured a ride to Fresno.

Caught in an Autumn Snowstorm
on the Summit of University Peak

LEAVING THE UPPER MARGIN of the piedmont slope east of the southern Sierra Nevada, I began to trudge up a trail to Kearsarge Pass on the crest of the range. Within a few hours I stood on the pass. Wishing to ascend Mt. Gould immediately to the north, I followed a ridge to its summit, 13,001 feet in elevation. I enjoyed a superb panorama of mountain, valley, and desert perhaps a hundred miles in radius.

The sky was clear except for a few clouds above the distant western horizon. I descended some distance in northwesterly direction until I intersected a ridge running west from the main crest of the range. Reaching a saddle in the latter I clambered up a ridge to the slightly lower summit of Mt. Rixford. Leaving this summit and continuing along the ridge, I climbed a third unnamed peak.

By this time great masses of clouds that had swept up from the distant western horizon glowed crimson and gold in the rays of the setting sun. I hurried down the south slope of the mountain, but by the time I reached Bullfrog Lake, an altitude of some 10,500 feet, the sky had become completely overcast, threatening an imminent storm. Continuing down the trail as it switchbacked southward to Vidette Meadow, I reached camp some time after nightfall.

At dawn the sky was clear, but a wall of cloud extending along the western horizon flushed pink. After breakfast I began to ascend Vidette Creek eastward toward Center Basin. The sharp pyramid of the East Vidette seen through a screen of foxtail pines against a background of clouds formed a very striking picture. As I began to ascend the western slopes of University Peak, the clouds disappeared and long morning shadows extended westward from peaks on the crest of the Sierra.

Upon reaching a somewhat higher altitude, however, I saw a great cloud bank reaching over the crest of the Coast Range, stretching eastward across the wide valley of the San Joaquin and already slowly creeping up the west slope of the Sierra. A storm was approaching. Onward came the mass of clouds with

117

now and then detached fragments appearing before it, like scouts before an advancing army.

Although the summit of University Peak was still some 2,000 feet above, I decided to attempt to reach it before the approaching storm should overtake me. Hurrying up a ridge which soon broke into a jagged arête, I climbed onto the top of the mountain 13,588 feet above the sea. As I looked to the north and south long cloud-fingers poured over the peaks on the main crest of the range. Silently, menacingly, but beautifully, the whirling mass of vapor advanced. Although there was no rumble of thunder, no flash of lightening, nor inky-hued clouds, within an hour the mountain would be enveloped in a blinding snowstorm.

There was no time to tarry on the summit of University Peak. I struck out eastward along the summit arête until I reached a route running down the north face to a cirque in which lie the Matlock Lakes. Most of the way down I travelled knee-deep in snow. The fog soon became so dense that I could not see more than fifty yards; presently it turned to snow.

As I continued to pick way way through the falling snow and over chaotically strewn boulders, I reached the Matlock Lakes. Pressing onward below the lakes in the direction of the Kearsarge Pass Trail, I temporarily emerged from the snow clouds. But as I came to the trail and hurried eastward along it, the storm continued to roll slowly down from the crest of the Sierra. The mountains loomed obscurely above the lakes; flying snow eddied about the foxtail pines as the wind soughed mournfully through them, singing the diapason of winter. Perhaps it was time for it to do so, for this was the first of November.

I kept pretty well below the oncoming storm, until finally I reached my car. The storm proved the precursor of a succession of storms which continued for days. When the cloud masses eventually cleared away, the great rampart of the Sierra rose white from base to summit.

Snowbound in the Sierra Nevada

For TEN YEARS AND MORE I have spent my winters in the Sierra Nevada, usually at an elevation of some 8,000 feet, snowbound for an average of four months of the year. Except for the regular two or three trips of the snow surveyors, my visitors have been few and far between. Despite the present mania for skiing, the average skier seldom goes a mile from a ski lift. Except for a very limited number of localities the snow-clad high Sierra throughout the winter, in fact throughout the spring also, is still very much of a *terra incognita*.

I was very much surprised in reading "The Wilderness of Denali" to learn that its author, Charles Sheldon, who spent a winter in a cabin of his own construction a few miles north of Mt. McKinley and over a hundred miles from the nearest settlement had more visitors during a single winter than I have had during several. Although my present winter headquarters is but eleven miles from El Camino Sierra and some 275 miles from Los Angeles, for months during the winter seldom does anyone ascend that far from the valley. My cabin is only a vertical mile above it, but to most a vertical mile, unless it can be travelled on wheels, is more than a hundred horizontal ones. Perhaps my solitary manner of life is one that I have drifted into rather than definitely chosen. As I sometimes jokingly remark, "I have been an *homme détaché* so long that I will not have civilization, nor will civilization have me."

"But how do you spend your time, so much of it?" many people ask. I am well aware that for many people who know of no better way to employ their time than to play solitaire, this would indeed be a problem. For someone, however, who has more hobbies than he can keep abreast of, the problem is not so much having too much free time, but rather not having enough. With reading and writing, taking pictures, occasional practice with rifle and pistol, and during the months of deep snow, rather frequent ski trips to timberline and beyond, I have more than ample use for all the spare time at my disposal.

Most of the higher portions of the Sierra Nevada, during

119

three-fourths of the year, are a detached world looking far down upon the populated one. High up in the range here and there is the isolated cabin of a watchman in charge of the flow of water for some power company, but these are few and far between. There are also some winter sport lodges, but few of their visitors travel any great distance from them. In fact, before the leaves of the deciduous trees have fallen, except for a scattering of deer hunters, the greater portion of the higher Sierra Nevada has been completely deserted by its summer sojourners and transient visitors. The traveller in the high Sierra throughout the winter and spring is almost as isolated as if he were in the sub-Arctic or even in the Arctic region, so far as encountering persons from without the mountains is concerned.

A part of the fascination in dwelling for months of the year in such location of the Sierra is that I enjoy some of the romance of the far north without actually being remote from civilization. Here at 8,000 feet above the sea in the Canadian Zone I enjoy deep snow without extremely low temperature. Seldom does the thermometer drop more than a few degrees below zero. If I so desire, I can snap on my skis and within several hours be well up into the Hudsonian Zone. Several more hours will put me in the Arctic-Alpine Zone beyond the last trees. I frequently ascend to timberline and return within a single day. In fact, although snowbound high in the Sierra for months at a time, thanks to my skis, I am never actually so.

Sierra foothills from Baker Creek Ranch, April 1970.

Sorting manuscripts at . . .

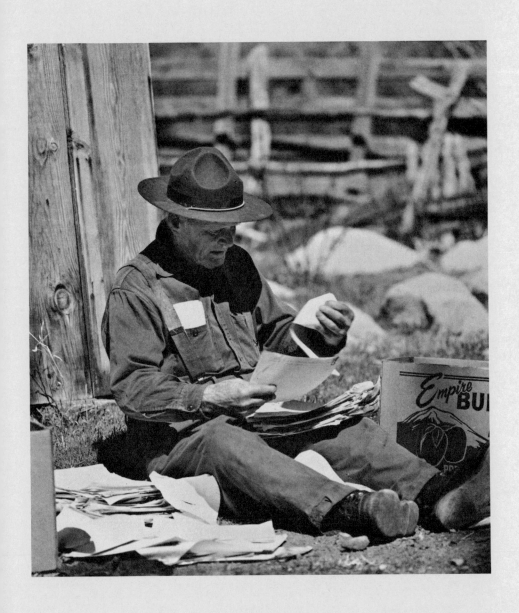

Baker Creek Ranch, April 1970

Jules Eichorn with Clyde, Baker Creek Ranch, April 1970.

*Four photographs of the Old Gaffer at his last Basecamp,
Fourth Recess, August 8, 1970.*

When I was talking about campaign hats I forgot to mention Norman's other hats and caps. When a man is such a character in both senses of the word, and bears on his crown such a distinguishing advertisement for such a portion of a whole century, it is positively startling to see that shock of unruly white hair escaping from under a stocking cap or a ski cap or a fedora. I'm only exaggerating a little if I say there might be a fez, also, in his pack.

Walt Wheelock mentions that Norman's first ascent cairns are found all over the Sierra, by bold climbers who think they are first to reach a rock summit. Harold Klieforth and I came upon one in the early 1960's, with no record other than Norman's for thirty years before our arrival. I think it may be, too, that Norman did not mark all his first ascents by the customary erection of a stone monument, or even comment on the feat. In more recent years, Norman has been going with the Sierra Club as a kind of king of the woodpile and general storyteller, and a sort of museum exhibition, being, as he says, "about nine hundred years old." This story is a joke on himself and a reminiscence reaching back to the dim past.

I have followed Norman on innumerable short walks and watched him build his famous green log fireplace campsites in many a wilderness bivouac, panted up his snowsteps, shinnied up his rock routes, and skied far back in his wake across the glacier, but I thought the time I invited him to go with me on a cattle-hauling trip across Nevada I would surely catch him off base. Hauling cattle in a truck and trailer is a hot, dusty, noisy, tiresome grind across dirt roads throughout the endless desert wastes, but Norman sat stoically across the cab from me for the whole thirty-hour trip, in apparent enjoyment and appreciation of the scene. My proud manipulation of the rig impressed him not the least, but he had many comments on the sparse vegetation and scattered wildlife of the steppes whenever the engine noise permitted. Whoever calls him taciturn does not know our friend well or needs a thesaurus. Mostly the frequent stops to check on the cows, the loading and unloading, etc., reminded my companion of his time spent on cattle ranches and a flood of memories ensued, unfortunately all lost in the fogs of my poor memory.

The other day Doug Robinson and I went down to Big Pine to check up on Norman, where he lives in an old house at the rear of the Sanitorium grounds. He is there because he has been

raided by the hoodlum kids of Big Pine of the very necessities
of life, including the bare equipment for survival; his pots and
pans and kerosene pressure lamps for reading, his axes and
wedges. He estimates it would cost one hundred fifty dollars to
replace his stores to living conditions again, and that is the
money he has been trying to save up out of his county pension
for a car. Of course, he should not have a car at all, because he
is really a hazard to himself and others. His reaction times have
slowed and his one eye and one ear are not quite up to the increased speeds of modern traffic. On the other hand, here is a
man who has lived at least fifty years in total independence,
and now he is subjected to the insulting and degrading position
of being waited on by well-meaning but impersonal nurses, who
have rules and regulations and their own ideas about what is
the proper temperature for a reading room, and when lights
should be on and off, and whether smoking should be permitted
—and horrors, even smoke themselves and puff the air even
fouler with vapors medicinal and poisonous, and do not guard
him from garrulous vapidities . . . and with a car he could stock
his old cabin at Baker Ranch with groceries, drive to Bishop
for the advantages of the big city, make that long-delayed trip
to the Last Chance Range, and once again be in business for
himself.

So the three of us drove up to the old ranch, which is really
only a mile from the Sanitorium. This time he did not make a
very pointed effort to show us the outdoor living room—fifty
yards from the old, vine-covered three-room ranch house, where
he has dragged four old davenports from the town dump and
arranged them in a circle—in order to dissuade us from entering the unkempt house. I knew that the reason he could let me in,
and even Doug, who was a stranger, was that all the incredible
mess of total chaos could be blamed on the looters. And indeed,
it was terrible. Cardboard grocery boxes full of photographs,
lantern slides, drawings, magazines, writings, articles, notes,
and all the paperwork a part-time professional nature writer
might collect in a half century, were no longer stacked to the
ceiling around the walls of the three small rooms of Mrs.
Baker's old house, but now lay strewn across the floors like a
cartoonist's drawing of an earthquake. I thought I could feel
through my boots the slick texture of photographic paper which,
I could not help realizing, bore images of mountain scapes re-
corded as incidentals of high and dangerous adventure, in a

130

spirit of noble sportsmanship probably inconceivable to the vandals responsible for such outrage. But I knew, from rare previous glimpses into the pack rat décor of Norman's boar's nest, that only the worst of the disarray was caused by forces beyond Norman's control. He was never a neat man. Perhaps he wanted to be, or meant to be. I suspect his intellectual turn of mind predisposed him to a regard for order, but he was most unorderly and, if my theory is correct, this is what made his failing really hurt. Perhaps because it would wound his fierce pride, he almost never allowed anyone to see the inside of his house.

It puzzles me, now that I think about it, that the cabins he occupied during the winters at Glacier Lodge could be so all-fired cluttered. After all, there be only so much crap a man can lug into a one-room cabin, to mess up in only one winter. You remember that every summer he had to get out. Nevertheless, those cabins were a weird and wonderful display of the largest one-man Seattle Co-op mountain equipment store I've ever seen. I think he never in his life threw out anything, and he was convinced that there was at least one right and proper piece of equipment for every conceivable situation that might ever happen to a man in the mountains, and he believed in having it ready to hand and, if possible, in duplicate.

Just starting from the ground up and not wishing to go into extreme detail, I might call your attention to the different types of slippers one can find advertised in the Sears & Sawbuck catalogue. It is a good idea to have the slipper with just a toepiece and no heel, because they are the fastest to put on, but then, they are a little cold, so later on in the winter one wants a warmer model, with heels, and as the temperature really drops it is nice to have sheepskin-lined slippers, and for awhile one could get cheap, war surplus aviator boots with rubber soles and sheep lining, but the leather deteriorated after awhile, and the straps were generally taken off to repair snowshoe bindings. Then too, if some hungry coyote comes 'round just asking to be shot, and it's one of those real, frosty-frozen crusted nights, then it's best to have a slipper that's quickly thrown on and still has a good, nonskid sole, maybe an old Bramani hand-sewed on . . . I still have not even got off the ground, but you get the idea.

There is a photograph of the old Glacier Lodge cabin on our bulletin board here now, as I write, and it reminds me of

131

a couple of things. The picture shows me arriving at the cabin on skis, with a hundred-pound sack of potatoes on my back. I've kept the old picture all these years because it is completely out of character, and the only time I've ever carried one hundred pounds on skis, but it was nothing at all out of the ordinary for Norman and was exactly how he got his supplies into the then-isolated house in the little grove of Jeffreys in Big Pine Canyon. No, it was seldom a case of transporting such awful loads all the way up the eleven miles and four thousand feet from Big Pine, but anything which wasn't hauled in before snow time did have to arrive by muscle power from wherever the snowline on the un-plowed road stopped the old Chevrolet. Also, he would go down to Big Pine for his mail several times during the winter, which would occasionally involve making the entire trip on foot. I don't think he ever had a regular schedule for mail trips, be-cause it seems to me that time I visited him, when he complained of almost losing his power of speech, was after a five-month absence from the valley.

The cabin in the canyon there was deep in a grove of big trees, but one window—the one at his bed—offered a day and night view of the most spectacular peak standing boldly at the head of the canyon. This beautiful mountain had long been call-ed, by those geography freaks who have to identify every spire in the Sierra Nevada, Peak 13,659. However, for at least three decades now it has been known as Clyde Peak, because Nor-man was the first to climb it, and because of all Norman's first ascents, it is the one mountain which dominated his cabin and in some ways his life for a quarter century. He could watch the topmost crags turn pink from the morning sun while still in his bed, and all day long he would turn and gaze at it from time to time, and its starlit snows still gleamed faintly in the clear Sierra skies when he doused the lantern at night.

Probably a startling proportion of all the photographs he has taken are of this noble peak, taken either from his front window or from pine-leaf-framed viewpoints nearby. Rumor has it that the name Clyde Peak is in the archives of the U.S. Board on Geographic Names, and that new maps will eventually so honor Norman Clyde. I certainly hope they will also follow the custom of Palisade mountaineers in designating the two glaciers situated on the mountain as East Clyde and North Clyde Glaciers. Fortunately they are visible from some favored spots in the Owens Valley and eastern ranges, and frame a rock peak

132

which is rather difficult to climb. An appropriate mountain to carry Norman's name, no doubt. Its elevation, just short of the nearby fourteen-thousand-foot Middle Palisade, guards it from the ravages of the multitude and, like Norman, its visage suggests the adjectives—prominent yet unknown, wild, aloof, dignified, difficult.

Norman was never really what I would call a close friend. Actually, I never had anybody in just this relation to me. He was about thirty years my senior for one thing, and a man of formidable reputation to one who for much of his life has made mountain climbing a chief excuse for living, and who heard of him first many years before encountering him, while still in the grip of romantic hero worship of the classic pioneers of our sport. But Norman turned out to be a sort of institution which we took for granted. He was always just part of the scene. We knew he could be found up there at the cabin on Big Pine Creek, or the old ranch on Baker Creek, ready to show us some newfangled aluminum slingshot he had just bought, or to walk three thousand feet up the mountainside for a color photograph of the wind-blown spring snow off the peaks, or an overnight trip to that high tarn where we could get on the cliff early enough in the morning to return for trout fishing, or that anyway he would sooner or later be around to dig into my library and scatter everything around the living room, and jam-and-butter-and-syrup-up the tablecloth and tell us of the summer high trip and how to load for a little more muzzle velocity.

Someone said once that Norman was open-ended, meaning, I suppose, that his life was "unstructured," as the current cliché has it. Not so. Not if the someone meant that Norman is the least bit unreliable, or inclined in the slightest to live a loose and unscheduled life. Possibly other people have made the same mistake in assuming that because Norman lives an unconventional life and dresses in outmoded clothes and seldom gets around to the barber, he may therefore be assumed to have the free and easy attitudes of hippies and others in our modern, liberated sub-cultures. Yet how he does fume when someone does not show up when they say they will! His famous temper can shoot above the flash point with explosive force at even the delayed receipt of expected mail. It is true he is not all that careful himself, and often loses his calendar and constantly loses his watch but, perhaps like the neatness he does not practice but still regards as appropriate, he really admires punctuality.

133

"Ringtail"

As WINTER APPROACHES a number of small animals, both furred and feathered, tend to gather about my cabin at an elevation of 8,000 feet above the sea on the east slope of the Sierra Nevada. Among these is a ringtail or *Bassariscus*, sometimes called a ringtailed cat although not related to the cat family in any respect. The ringtail is a slender animal with a grayish body tinged with a tawney hue on the back, averaging some fifteen inches in length and having a broad tail barred alternately black and white. Its general facial expression, and its large eyes with a double black and white band around them, cause considerable resemblance to the racoon, to which it is related. Like the racoon it is almost exclusively nocturnal in its habits, so much so that even in areas where the ringtail is fairly common it may be seldom or never seen by residents of that district. When it frequents buildings in quest of mice and rats, its comings and goings by dark are so stealthy that residents of the buildings do not notice it. Even when it raises a racket, as it sometimes does, the ringtail may be mistaken for a pack rat which indulges in similar commotions.

The *Bassariscus* is a carnivore whose food consists mainly of rats, mice, ground squirrels and similar small rodents, doubtless varied by an occasional bird. Its long, lithe body together with squirrel-like claws render it an agile climber and its long, fluffy tail aids it in making extremely long bounds. The ringtail's unusually large eyes are perhaps as good as those of the cat for seeing in the dark, and its large upright ears indicate very sensitive hearing. Nevertheless, the ringtail is a rather gentle animal. It has, for example, little of the ferocity which characterizes members of the weasel family, even its smallest species. When angry the ringtail spits, snarls and makes peculiar guttural sounds, but it sometives gives the impression that the more it does so, the less it feels inclined to fight.

If the ringtail chooses to frequent a building, especially a loft or attic, it comes to regard this as its own particular domain, and should other small animals of its own or other species intrude, they may be unceremoniously thrown out. These encounters, however, may be preceded by somewhat prolonged pre-liminaries in which the intruder, especially if this happens to be another ringtail, is informed by an extremely varied assortment of hisses, snarls and strange throaty sounds that its presence is not desired. These failing to produce the desired effect, a battle royal may follow. Other undesired intruders, especially the spotted skunk, may present a more difficult problem to the resident ringtail, for although the latter is easily able to eject the invader, the after-effects of such an encounter are not at all pleasant. Several times these small skunks have attempted to take possession of the attic of my cabin, already pre-empted by a ringtail. From its unusually long preliminaries, the ringtail always appears loath to enter into combat with such an enemy. Eventually, however, it must and succeeds in throwing the offender out. As there are several cracks in the celotex ceiling of my cabin, the aftermath of such battles drive me out for several days.

In the mountain ranges of California the habitat of the ringtail extends from areas close to sea level to an elevation of at least 8,000 feet. In summer they probably range at considerably higher altitudes. One is reported to have been trapped in mid-winter at about 11,000 feet in the southern Sierra, but this is exceptional, since their food consists of small rodents, most of which hibernate at higher elevations. Furthermore, the ringtail is not so well adapted to survive in deep snow as is the marten, for example. Although it has a good coat of fur during the winter months, its feet are not as heavily furred as the marten's and they are small in proportion to the weight of the ringtail's body. Hence it cannot run about so readily in deep soft snow, nor can it hunt so efficiently in such conditions. Even the well-equipped marten, with the gradual decrease of the food supply at higher elevations as winter advances, has some difficulty surviving. So far as my observations extend, 8,000 feet appears to be the upper limit at which an occasional ringtail remains throughout the winter in the southern Sierra Nevada. As a matter of fact, I doubt whether the one which takes up its abode in the attic of my cabin during the winter would remain in the vicinity were it not provided with some food during that season.

Although the coming and going of the ringtail to and from the attic of my cabin is always quiet and stealthy, its sojourn in the latter is not always so. It is fond of racing back and forth and sometimes, judging from the commotion it makes, of en-

135

gaging in some sort of solitary game of blind man's bluff; and, worse still, its favorite time for indulging such playful propensities appears to be 4:00 A.M., and that, usually directly over my bed. Sometimes for these reasons, added to its occasional battles with intruders, I feel disposed to exclude the ringtail from my attic, which could easily be done by closing several small apertures. But as it is a very interesting little animal, and because there is little wild life astir in the vicinity of my cabin in winter, I continue to permit it to engage in a battle now and then with other small animals and to indulge in such playful commotion as it is wont to do.

A Mid-Winter Ascent of Mt. Whitney, Highest Mountain in the Continental United States

ALTHOUGH FROM EARLY spring to late autumn I have climbed Mt. Whitney some fifty times and from almost every direction, I have done so but once in mid-winter. That was in January some years ago. After making my way on snowshoes to an elevation of 10,000 feet, I made camp on a bare spot on the lee of a large pine log. For one reason and another, I did not get under way the following morning until half past eight.

It was a long pull over the snow to Whitney Pass, 13,600 feet above the sea, on the crest of the Sierra, about two miles south of the summit of Mt. Whitney. From the pass the trail runs northward a short distance below and west of the crest, past Mt. Muir (14,025 feet) and onward past the base of a succession of pinnacles sometimes called the Shark's Teeth, and finally up a rise of several hundred feet to the rather spacious and gently inclining summit of Mt. Whitney. During winter high winds usually sweep most of the snow from the trail between the pass and the top of the mountain, except in spots where it may be piled in drifts. The snow in these drifts is generally packed so hard that it may be necessary to cut steps with an ice axe to get around it safely. During this stretch of the trail, therefore, I had little need for snowshoes. In fact, I carried them most of the way.

As the traveling had been slow, I did not reach the summit until very late in the afternoon. It had been swept almost free of snow by winds, some of them no doubt of gale-like intensity. Far northward and slightly westward the eye followed the crest of the Sierra to the mountains of Yosemite Park upwards of a hundred miles distant; eastward it swept over desert plains and desert mountains to the Panamint Range, beyond which lies Death Valley. My thermometer read twelve degrees above zero, mild temperature for that time of day and elevation. The reason was not far to seek. To the west a great mass of dense vapor was slowly creeping up the slope of the Sierra.

Tarrying but a few minutes on the top of Mt. Whitney, I began the return making fairly good speed. As I neared Mt.

137

Muir, however, the cloud-mass was sweeping overhead, and with it, heavy wind and flying snow. I cast about for a way to escape. Not far ahead was a couloir or steep chute on the east side of the crest, up and down which I had rather frequently passed on ascents of the mountain during spring and summer. Reaching its head, I began to make my way down it, but the snow in the chute had been packed so hard by wind that it was necessary to cut steps. Doing this down a steep couloir at any time is a rather laborious procedure. It was especially so at night in the midst of a mid-winter storm.

For upwards of a thousand feet I patiently cut my way down, eventually emerging from the lower end of the couloir onto a steep slope buried deep with snow. By that time the storm had relented somewhat. On snowshoes again, I continued down the steep slope. Camp was still several miles distant; moonlight filtering through the flying clouds assisted me appreciably as I made my way toward it.

At 1:20 A.M. I arrived. As well may be imagined, I was not long in crawling into my sleeping bag to the lee of the great prostrate log.

Snowslides in the Sierra Nevada

SNOWSLIDES ARE A FREQUENT occurrence in the Sierra Nevada although not nearly so common nor so grand in scale as those in the high mountains of more northerly latitudes. They happen most often between midwinter and spring during or just after a heavy snowfall, particularly when snow has built up on a steeply inclining frozen surface. With little to adhere to, masses of snow need slight encouragement to go sweeping down a mountainside.

In a season of unusually heavy snowfall—fifteen feet of snow fell within two weeks—a party of us engaged in a snow survey came upon a mile-wide strip on the headwater of Bubbs Creek which had been swept by a snowslide. The snow had simply peeled off and avalanched down to the bottom of the canyon, carrying with it many trees and rocks, burying and shattering a number of buildings on the canyon floor. While on our trip we observed a number of smaller slides on the opposite side of the canyon. Where the slope was continuous they swept down in great white sheets. Usually, however, they leaped over cliffs, forming beautiful snowfalls. As they came darting down a chute, plunging at intervals over drop-offs, their resemblance to foaming waterfalls was very striking.

In the same year late in May slides were numerous on the headwaters of the Middle Fork of the Kaweah River. From my camp at an elevation of 9,000 feet I saw a number every day, most commonly in late afternoon when the snow had been loosened by the warm sunshine. A rather spectacular and unusual one occurred on the opposite side of the canyon. I heard a dull rumbling of rocks as I was preparing dinner, and turned around to observe the head of a snowslide emerging from the mouth of a chute about two hundred yards distant. Great chunks of snow and occasional rocks were coming down with a motion as much rolling as sliding, the whole mass gradually slowing up, eventually coming to rest along the slope of the canyon.

The rolling motion of snowslides appears to be the reason why persons caught in them are likely to be sucked in. While descending a mountain in this vicinity I had such an experience.

Weary of forcing my way through the snow into which I sank knee-deep, I decided to start a slide and ride it down the mountainside. As the upper layer of snow was rather recent it was not firmly amalgamated to the crusted mass beneath, so that by merely sitting down on it heavily I could start a snowslide.

The manufactured slide began to move down the mountainside, at first with moderate speed. But when it came to an area which was completely in shadow where the surface was already frozen, it suddenly shot down with startling acceleration. The slide eventually slackened in speed, and by careful manipulation of my ice axe I was able to swing out of it. Not content with this experience, however, I presently started another. I checked my speed sufficiently for a huge rolling ball of snow to overtake me. It struck me on the back and knocked me sprawling. As I was shoved along, the sucking action of the snow, half sliding, half rolling, was very pronounced, but the speeding volume of snow was not sufficiently deep to do any harm except to half smother me. Eventually succeeding in regaining a sitting position, I continued along with the slide until I recovered my hat which for some distance had gone gaily bobbing up and down on the slide. I then worked my way diagonally along until the margin of the slide was reached. Since I was then near the head of a chute where the snow would be heaped up to a dangerous depth by confining walls, I indulged in no more freewheeling down the mountainside.

Snowslides in the Sierra may be divided into two classes: those which descend more or less open slopes, and those which go down steep, narrow chutes or couloirs. The latter are always dangerous; the former may or may not be. Provided that the slope below is uniform and the layer of sliding snow not too deep nor intermixed with rocks, little danger may attend riding them; there is a peculiar and fascinating sensation in being swept along by their gliding, serpentine motion. However, should anyone be caught in a snowslide of any consequence in a steep couloir, the experience is likely to prove fatal. A careful climber never will ascend or descend a snow-filled chute if there are any indications that a slide may occur. After a spring snow storm in the Sierra I have seen slide after slide come down the numerous couloirs on the precipitous fronts of the Palisades.

I have had only one narrow escape of this sort. On the northeast face of the Middle Palisade a high, sheer cliff springs up from a glacier. Above this, steep, trough-like chutes ascend to

140

the top of the mountain, an elevation of 14,040 feet at its highest point. On one of my ascents of this face of the peak, I mounted the initial cliff by climbing a sort of chimney to a notch in the rim. While observing a rather unusual formation of rock a few feet above the margin of the couloir, I heard a swishing sound. As I turned about, the lower end of a snowslide, gliding down the chute like a great white serpent, shot past me and poured down through the notch which I had come through a few minutes earlier. This slide was almost silent because it had few rocks. Generally, however, there are enough rocks intermingled with the snow to cause a rattling or even a crashing sound.

Slides of any magnitude, whether of snow or rock, are one of the things most feared by mountaineers. As there is no way to combat or control them, the best that can be done is to keep out of their way. As a rule, experienced mountaineers can judge by the condition of the snow whether there is any great likelihood of one occurring. In the case of couloirs, there is likely to be freshly fallen debris piled up at their lower ends, if slides have been taking place. In the Sierra Nevada in general snowslides occur during winter, spring, and early summer, depending on the snow conditions during any particular season. During summer and autumn, most of the slides which take place are more properly rock slides.

Up to the High Sierra Cirques
on Skis in Mid-Winter

THE JAGGED SUMMITS OF the Sierra Palisades, several of them more than 14,000 feet in elevation above the sea, glowed roseate in the light of dawn as I looked out of my cabin at 8,000 feet. I stepped out into a little glade among the birches and noticed that the thermometer stood at zero. But the atmosphere was so calm that it did not seem to be really cold. For several days previously the mountains had been swept by a heavy wind and enveloped in whirling masses of vapor. A north wind, however, had come up and cleared away the storm clouds. Now, as is usual in the Sierra in winter, a period of calm weather would follow, lasting perhaps a week, possibly several.

It was February and the snow already lay deep in the high basins and cirques immediately below the crest of the Sierra. With the recent fall of snow, doubtless in powder form, the skiing conditions in these should be excellent. I returned to my cabin; but an hour later I emerged again carrying my skis. Snapping them on, I began to glide up the almost level floor of the canyon through thickets of birch and willow, past numerous leafless cottonwoods and occasional tall, stalwart Jeffrey pines.

Within a few hundred yards I came to the foot of a stretch of cascades on the North Fork of Big Pine Creek. They came leaping sonorously down from a glacially formed basin, the first of a series forming a step and tread succession leading upward and westward to the great amphitheatre on the headwaters of the stream. After traversing the floor of this basin somewhat over a quarter of a mile in length, I switchbacked up a second step with a vertical rise of some 800 feet. At an elevation of 9,000 feet I was now well into the Canadian Zone. In the lower portion of the basin I passed many large Jeffrey pines, but as I continued these rapidly decreased both in numbers and in size and were succeeded by lodgepole and soon by occasional white-bark pines.

As I glided smoothly along in the powder snow I noticed the trails of numerous animals. Among others were those of the Douglas squirrel, active in the Sierra throughout the winter, ex-

142

cept during stormy periods, over a range that extends into the Hudsonian Zone to the last sizable trees. Here and there were the footprints of a weasel and the similar but much larger ones of the marten, the arch enemy of the Douglas squirrel. I saw larger tracks, not clearly defined, which might have been made by a wolverine, an animal that has been encountered on the headwaters of this stream.

Up a rather steep slope, through an open stand of pine and fir, and around the end of a bold spur I climbed in a zigzag course to the lower end of a wide draw up which I continued. At an elevation of some 10,000 feet I came abreast of First Lake, and then encountered a succession of lakes which occupy basins scooped out for them by a glacier now vanished. Southward across the lakes Temple Crag, an unusually beautiful peak, rose to an elevation of 12,999 feet. The skiing was excellent, except that in spots the recently fallen snow, exposed to sunshine, became so sticky that it adhered to the climbers attached to my skis and slowed down my speed.

Rising steadily I went over a brow, and continued westward across an undulating area clothed with stands of whitebark and lodgepole pines lying at an elevation of some 10,500 feet. Several Sierra grouse flew noisily from the pines on whose boughs they had been perching, absorbing the warm sunshine. In mid-winter at these elevations I seldom come upon the tracks of the grouse on the snow; they appear to spend most of their time in pine trees, subsisting upon their needles and perhaps buds. Now and then, however, they will suddenly burst out from the snow within a few yards—perhaps within a few feet—as I go skiing silently along. Sometimes they plunge into powder snow, burying themselves. As the snow affords excellent insulation this is a good maneuver provided that a crust does not form on the surface, or a prowling marten does not happen along that way.

After crossing a frozen lake and continuing over more undulating terrain, I swung around the end of a spur projecting southward from a high ridge. As I did so I came within full view of the spacious amphitheatre on the headwaters of the North Fork. Southeastward across it, several miles distant, the bold form of Mt. Sill rose steeply to an elevation of 14,162 feet; directly southward the North Palisade rose to 14,242 in the highest of several spiry peaks which surmount its narrow crest. Beyond the end of the spur I crossed another frozen lake and

143

then climbed to the top of a bluff several hundred feet high. The encircling snow-clad mountains, overarched by a cloudless azure sky, were beautiful. Numerous knolls in the vicinity were clothed with whitebark pines which cast blue shadows across dazzling white snow.

After a halt of somewhat over a half hour spent in eating luncheon, waxing my skis and surveying the magnificent surrounding scenery, I again snapped on my skis. I ran obliquely downward for a few hundred yards, swung around the end of the spur and continued eastward across the undulating area, enjoying numerous short but enjoyable runs in powder snow in the open stand of whitebark pines, to the brow of the rather steep slope up which I had come in the morning. Exposed to the sunshine during the middle hours of the day, the surface of the snow had frozen and upon it a crust had now formed as afternoon shadows crept down the slopes. This presented some difficulty as one knee had not fully recovered from a sprain incurred during a badly coordinated open Christiania turn several weeks previously. It was therefore with considerable caution that I swung back and forth over the crusted snow down through an open stand of pines. Eventually I came to the lower margin of the pine-clad area and entered the head of a long draw where the snow was free from crust. I sped swiftly along in the powder snow on the gentler inclination of the floor of the main canyon which I soon reached. I clattered along in the frozen ski tracks which I had made in the morning.

Down the floor of the basin I continued for a mile or more when my somewhat reckless running was suddenly brought to a halt by the brow of the second step which I had ascended that morning. I had hoped that this would be entirely covered with powder snow, in which case, steep as it was, it would afford an unusually fine run. To my disappointment, however, the upper portion was heavily crusted. With only one good knee, I found this somewhat disconcerting. I made my way cautiously down for several hundred feet, when I was agreeably surprised to come upon snow in fine powder condition down the remainder of the step. I swooped and continued down the gently inclining floor of the tread immediately below it for perhaps a half mile.

As I was approaching the brow of the first step I descried some distance ahead what appeared to be the shadow of a pine tree cast upon the snow, for the moon was now shining brightly. When almost upon it, however, I discovered that it was not a

144

shadow but a patch of bare ground. Too late either to swerve or to stop, I crouched, hoping to be able to charge across. It proved to be strewn with broken rock and upon striking it, I was catapulted through the air fifteen or twenty feet. I picked myself up intact, my injured knee none the worse for the tumble; I had not suffered a scratch. Providence, I said, really looks after people belonging to a certain none-too-complimentary category.

After gathering up ski poles and hat, I descended the first step, several hundred feet in height, and continued along the gently inclining floor of the basin below it. The moon, now nearing the full, was shining brightly as I threaded my way past Jeffrey pines, cottonwoods lining the stream, and birch trees overarching it. Soon I reached the door of my cabin, having enjoyed an unusually fine trip entailing an ascent of some 3,500 feet. Despite my flying, headlong leap I was none the worse for the somewhat wild ski run on the return.

Climbing Hurd Peak on Skis

"HAVING CLIMBED MOST OF the higher peaks of the Sierra by the usual methods, why don't you set out to do so again on skis?" once remarked a well-known mountaineer to me. Being none too skillful on skis at the time, I paid little attention to this suggestion. Eventually, however, I decided that, if for no other reason than the novelty of the thing, I would ascend at least some of the mountains in this way. It should be understood at the outset, however, that my skis do not always actually reach the top of the mountain. Generally they are left some distance below and the final ascent accomplished with the aid of ice axe and nailed boots. Among the summits which I have reached in this fashion is Hurd Peak, a sharply pyramidal peak 12,224 feet in elevation on the headwaters of the South Fork of Bishop Creek.

Leaving Parcher's Camp, an elevation of some 9,000 feet, about the middle of March, I skied up the last mile and a half of the road then buried beneath many feet of snow. Beyond this, I continued southward, following for some distance the general course of the trail leading to Bishop Pass. As I rounded a promontory above South Lake the snow was frozen so hard and the slope so steep that I removed my skis and negotiated some two hundred yards of mountainside in boots provided with tricouni nails, this being easier and safer than forcibly slamming the edges of the skis into the hard crust.

Presently I entered an open stand of lodgepole and white-bark pine where the snow was in powder form. Up steep slopes I switchbacked to and fro among the pines, eventually passing over a brow to an undulating terrain cut up by numerous narrow ravines. Hurd Peak, from this angle a sharp and handsome mountain, was then in plain view little more than a mile distant in an air-line, while to the right stood a number of high, snow-mantled peaks, the group describing a pronounced curve around the headwaters of Bishop Creek.

Sometimes traversing along steep slopes, at others swinging around the heads of narrow canyons, I eventually came to the foot of a precipitous slope, up which I zigzagged, striking the edges of my skis into the hard windboard or marble crust, as snow packed extremely hard by the wind is termed by skiers. Beyond the brow several frozen lakes came within view. Deeply buried in snow, they sunk in the middle of the great drifts about their margins, presenting a very different aspect than that seen during the summer months by devotees of the flycasting rod. To the left rose the Inconsolable Range, much of it too steep to afford lodgment for the snow, and swept nearly clean by heavy winds. In general, however, the surrounding mountains were heavily mantled with snow.

After crossing the outlet of Long Lake, I began to switch-back up a steep slope leading up to Hurd Peak. For some distance the powder snow was in excellent condition, but this was presently succeeded by hard windboard on a gradually steepening incline. Up this I swung back and forth in long switchbacks until within a short distance of the foot of the rocks on the actual face of the mountain, where I changed to nailed boots. To obviate the possibility of my skis being swept away by a snowslide during my absence, I carried them up and placed them at the base of a rock. A slide had already come down a wide chute to the right, and the afternoon sunshine was so warm that another might follow.

Because of the possibility of a slide, I avoided the couloirs in favor of a sort of rib on which many rocks projected above the snow. So warm fell the sunshine on the face of the mountain that the snow was soft and in many places I sank to my waist, occasionally even to my armpits, especially where there happened to be a cavity alongside a rock or underneath a clump of dwarf pine. When several hundred feet below the crest of the mountain I regretted having veered from the rib to the chute on the left, for the snow was so soft on the steep inclination that my weight could easily start a slide. I protected myself from such a contingency by keeping in line with the occasionally projecting rocks and eventually reached the bare rocks of the crest in safety.

Along this—a narrow and somewhat jagged knife edge—I picked my way northward for several hundred feet to its termination, the highest rock on the mountain. Up the narrow, vertical blade of granite I clambered *à cheval* fashion, pausing for a few minutes to admire the view.

From the southeast, where Mt. Agassiz, 13,891 feet in elevation occupies the foreground with the summits of Mt. Sill and the North Palisade peering over it, the crest of the Sierra curves around northwestward in a sweeping arc, along which stand a striking array of bold, cliff-walled peaks with mesa-like summits, together with an intermingling of sharp pyramids. The floor of the amphitheatre and all but the steepest cliffs and spires of mountains were buried deep in a mantle of stainless snow, down which the afternoon shadows were already creeping.

Not being especially eager to precipitate a snowslide in the descent, I decided to go down on the rocks. After following a knife edge eastward for a short distance, I proceeded to descend the south face. Although precipitous, the climbing was not really dangerous or difficult. Somewhat to my surprise, I presently detected the pleasant odor of the horkelia, one of the higher growing alpine plants. Scarcely had the snow disappeared from the face of the cliffs than this hardy little perennial had begun to show signs of awakening life.

After a descent of about five hundred feet on the rocks, I crossed the head of a couloir to the rib which I had followed in the ascent. This was gained without mishap, but to my annoyance, I suddenly dropped shoulder deep into a cavity below a rock. After extricating myself, I waded, plunged and on several occasions, wallowed down to the point at which I had left my skis. To avoid switchbacking, I carried the skis down the mountainside for a few hundred feet across the hard, smooth windboard. When I did eventually wish to avail myself of a little "freewheeling" I found the climbing socks frozen so firmly to the skis that they could not be removed. I therefore walked down to the lower end of Long Lake where the sun was still shining. There I placed them on a space of bare ground and within a few minutes had the satisfaction of removing the socks with ease.

The return to camp was one of unalloyed pleasure. Down slope after slope I went swooping along, darting in and out among trees, shooting down steep slopes out onto gently inclining flats. On the precipitous mountainside where I had worn nailed shoes in the morning the snow had become loosely granular from being exposed for hours to warm sunshine. Down this I coasted diagonally, keeping my speed well under control. Presently I was gliding along the trail in summer trodden by rider and pedestrian. I continued down the road, arriving a few minutes later in camp, thus ending a thrilling and somewhat adventurous day in the snowy Sierra.

148

An Enjoyable Climb to the Crest of the Sierra and Thrilling Return on Skis

M<small>Y SLEEPING BAG WAS</small> snugly ensconced in a cave-like recess beneath a dense-branched whitebark pine at an elevation of slightly over 11,000 feet on the headwaters of Rock Creek. It looked southward onto a small meadow surrounded by pine-clad undulations. Although the meadow was free from snow and grass and alpine flowers were already springing up, and although it was the 29th of May, snow still lay deep on the surrounding terrain. A hundred yards to the north lay Long Lake, still almost entirely covered with ice. A number of bold and beautiful mountains encircle its basin. The highest of these, Mt. Morgan, 13,748 feet in elevation, stands to the northeast; to the west, Mt. Mills (13,468 feet), Mt. Abbot (13,715 feet), and Mt. Dade (13,600 feet) form a striking array of peaks. The finest of these is Bear Creek Spire, a sculptured pyramidal peak, with an altitude of 13,705 feet, standing on the crest of the Sierra.

I had come up from the valley to enjoy a week or so of skiing and climbing. As I looked out from the snug recess the first rays of the rising sun glowed roseate on the sharp summit of Bear Creek Spire. Within a few minutes these changed to bright amber and began to creep down the sheer north face of the mountain. The sky was cloudless and seemed to promise a perfect day on the snow-clad mountains.

"It will be too fine a day," I thought, "to remain in camp." I therefore crawled out of my sleeping bag and began to prepare breakfast on a ranger-type fireplace in front of my *boudoir*, as I called it.

Breakfast over, after attaching a rucksack to a packboard upon which I had lashed a pair of six-foot skis in an upright position, I picked up my ice axe and began to follow a small coulee-like draw southward among the pine-clad undulations. The floor of the draw was buried in snow which had frozen so hard overnight that it would support my weight, so I wore climbing boots provided with sharp tricouni nails which bit into the frozen surface.

Within several hundred yards the draw intersected a canyon ascending southward to a bowl-like cirque lying at the northern base of Bear Creek Spire. Up this I continued and after climbing a rather steep rise of perhaps 800 feet, I came to a widening of the floor among the last trees where there were several snow-covered lakes. Here I came upon the tracks of a very large coyote. Even in mid-winter, if the snow is packed sufficiently firmly to support their weight, these animals will range beyond the last trees. In spring, when the winter snow usually forms a firm pack, they range far and wide over the higher portions of the Sierra, sometimes crossing passes more than 13,000 feet in elevation, in pursuit of various rodents and other small forms of wild life found at those elevations. They prey upon the Sierra hare throughout winter, and in spring, the marmot when it emerges from burrows in which it has hibernated perhaps six months.

Above the small lake basin I emerged from the narrow head of the canyon into the cirque lying immediately below the sheer north face of Bear Creek Spire. Southwestward across the gently rising floor I continued. In places this was covered with great numbers of dead and benumbed insects strewn about on the surface, borne thither doubtless by strong upward currents of air. As usual on such occasions a number of rosy finches were hopping about busily feeding upon them. Several times I came upon the feathers of a small bird scattered on the snow, apparently those of an Audubon warbler. Caught in a snowstorm these had probably been driven down into the snow-buried basin, perished, and their bodies devoured by a small roving predator, most likely a marten. These little carnivores sometimes climb over the snow to elevations over 14,000 feet in the southern Sierra.

To the north of Bear Creek Spire the cirque rises steeply to the crest of the Sierra, there an altitude of about 13,000 feet. The summit of this would, I thought, afford an excellent view, and the snow, a fine run down to the floor of the cirque when its surface had thawed sufficiently to form a thin granular layer.

I therefore switchbacked upward a thousand feet to the narrow crest. Westward I looked down into Lake Italy basin completely surrounded, except to the south, by high mountains. Its floor, almost entirely above timberline, was still buried underneath snow, and Lake Italy, lying midway along its floor, was covered with ice. After enjoying the view for some time, I removed the six-foot skis and ski poles from the packboard, and a pair of ski boots from the rucksack, and within a few minutes I was ready to begin the descent.

Warm sunshine had been shining for hours on the steep, eastward-facing slope. Instead of a layer of granular snow there was upwards of a foot lying on hard packed snow underneath. The surface had, in fact, thawed beyond the granular stage into what skiers sometimes term spring snow. This layer needed little in the way of encouragement to peel off and slide, slow at first but gradually gaining speed coursing downward to the floor of the cirque. I therefore switchbacked back and forth, and as I ran diagonally downward, even if the layer of snow began to peel off, I was elsewhere before it could carry me along. Within several hundred feet I reached the lower margin of the unstable snow, and freeing the brakes as it were, swung down the floor of the cirque in a curving course.

The lower margin of the latter reached, I shot down the narrow head of the canyon, then followed the alternating step and tread formation of the floor of the canyon. Past the lakes and then down the long, steep drop I continued, until a short distance below the latter, I swung to the right into the narrow draw, down which I continued through the open stand of pines to my camp.

It was about noon when I swung to a stop. I had an enjoyable climb over the snow to the crest of the Sierra, there slightly over 13,000 feet in elevation, and a thrilling run down a long, steep slope to the floor of the cirque and thence down several miles of a canyon to my camp among the pine-clad undulations in the zone immediately below timberline.

"Shadows lay across the glacier, its freezing surface crunched beneath the impact of our nailed boots, but the light of the declining sun fell athwart the jagged summits of the North Palisade. Presently it assumed an amber hue which soon deepened to a vivid rose. This, in turn, faded and the mountains became enveloped in the darkness of night."

The First Ascent Directly Up the North Face
of the North Palisade

THERE IS NO MORE spectacular peak in the Sierra Nevada, none more alluring to the mountaineer, than the North Palisade. It rises to an elevation of 14,242 feet above sea level among other peaks almost as high and almost as rugged. Its ascent was probably more of a problem than that of any other of the higher peaks of the Sierra. Only after considerable reconnaissance and repeated efforts was a route found up its south face by Joseph LeConte, Jr. Its northern face was long regarded as impossible, but eventually a way was found up a steep snow chute, over the broken wall of a cliff, and along a ragged knife edge to the summit.

Often I had scanned this face of the mountain for a more direct route. Only one seemed possible and that was dubious. It led up a narrow, snow-filled couloir for several hundred feet, thence up the face of the mountain for a few hundred more, and finally over broken cliffs to the summit. There were two places which might render it impracticable: the first was the couloir, because of the bergschrund below it and the steepness of the ice which filled it, and the second was the face of the mountain above, which appeared too sheer to afford sufficient holds for its ascent. Even repeated study of this route with binoculars failed to convince me of the feasibility of either of these portions.

However, one morning early in July I decided to make an attempt. Leaving camp on the Big Pine Lakes, I traversed a grassy basin and went over several miles of rocky acclivities above it to the border of the North Palisade Glacier which sweeps up to the base of the North Palisade and Mt. Sill to the left and Mt. Winchell to the right. The morning was extremely beautiful. The craggy peaks stood silhouetted against a stainless blue sky; blue shadows cast by their turreted summits rested on the snowy expanse of the glacier. Almost directly opposite was the steep couloir up which I hoped to make my way. Trudging steadily across the snow I reached the bergschrund at its base, fortunately to find a bridge of snow and ice across it. In one leap I reached its center and in another landed on the upper lip of the crevasse. Some step cutting carried me across a strip of glare ice to a steep snow slope, up which I continued for perhaps two hundred feet by kicking in my toes. For several hundred more I forced my way along the icy margin of the couloir and along the rock wall above it.

Discovering what promised to be a way up the portion of the face to my right which had appeared dubious from below, I hoisted myself up to it. Greatly to my surprise, I found it traversed by rather numerous horizontal ledges up which I zigzagged without any great difficulty. After several hundred feet of such scrambling, I found myself forced into the icy tongue of the couloir. Cutting my way across this, I began to lift myself up the steep but broken walls above it. There I encountered interesting and rather difficult climbing, but by veering to one side or another, was able to go around every obstacle which confronted me.

As I advanced, progress became more difficult because the way led up short, steep chimneys filled with loose snow underlain by smooth ice. To go forward, I was forced to scoop a trench in the snow with my ice axe and cut steps in the ice beneath it. In this way I pressed forward until immediately beneath the summit arête and only a few rods from the top of the mountain. There I was confronted by an overhanging rock. After trying in vain to hoist myself up by the scanty handholds available, I threw a rope over it and hauled myself over. A few minutes of scrambling then brought me to the summit, which was a narrow rock overhanging the steep north face up which I had climbed.

Throwing down my ice axe and rucksack, I began to survey the marvelous panorama of peaks commanded by the North Palisade, extending from Mt. Whitney in the south to the Yosemite in the north—an amazing array of lofty, snow-clad summits. Extending to the east and swinging to the northwest, the Palisade formed a great crescent with Mt. Sill and the Middle Palisade to the east and Mt. Winchell and Mt. Agassiz to the northwest. Beyond the latter were the rugged peaks of the Evolution Mountains, and beyond them and to the right the isolated and austere pyramid of Mt. Humphreys. The sky was almost cloudless and warm sunshine fell on my high perch. Several rosy finches flitted about.

After an hour's sojourn on the summit I began to descend. Wishing to avoid the icy chimneys just below the top, I followed

154

the summit-crest for a few hundred yards and then dropped from it to a snowfield on a moderately inclined slope, a remnant of an ancient landscape comparatively untouched by the forces of erosion. From this I swung northwesterly toward my route of the morning. I went too low, however, and was obliged to do some awkward traversing along shelves that dropped away to sheer cliffs. Eventually I reached the head of the couloir, crossed it to the ledges I had ascended and went down the chute. A considerable stream of water flower down it, sometimes underneath the ice, sometimes along its margin. By doing a good deal of hacking with my ice axe I cut my way over the ice, regardless of the stream, and was treated meanwhile to a generous wetting.

Presently I reached the foot of the couloir, leaped across the bergschrund, and glissaded down the steep upper slope of the glacier. Afternoon shadows fell across it, cast by the North Palisade, but the rays of the setting sun fell bright on the craggy face of Mt. Sill and an unnamed sharp peak to the north of it. I sped down the glacier and over the moraine, down the rocky slope to the green valley and thence over the rocks to my camp by the Big Pine Lakes.

The First Ascent of the Second Highest Peak
of the North Palisade

Whether from the standpoint of the lover of mountain scenery or the scaler of mountain peaks, the North Palisade is one of the most intriguing mountains of the Sierra Nevada. It rises in almost sheer walls to the north and the south, surmounted by several great pinnacles, the loftiest of which attains an elevation of 14,242 feet, the second highest, one of slightly over 14,000.

While making a number of ascents of the loftiest peak, I frequently gazed toward its somewhat lower neighbor several hundred yards to the northwest, wondering whether it too might not be scaled. Presenting the appearance of a sharp spire, its walls appear so sheer that adequate holds seemed to be lacking, and added to this was the fact that the actual summit is a tapering monolith thirty or more feet in height, which might demand rather arduous gymnastics to surmount it. During the summer of 1930, however, I suddenly decided to make an attempt.

Leaving camp at the Big Pine Lakes, an elevation of some 11,000 feet, one morning in early July, I descended to a meadow gay with a profusion of flowering *bryanthus*, cyclamen, arnica, asters, wild hellebore, and other flowers common to such locations. After traversing the meadow, I followed a trail leading southward to the North Palisade Glacier, somewhat over two miles distant. In the main, the trail followed a ridge to a point within about a half mile of the glacier. Upon coming to its termination, I crossed a stretch of glaciated rock several hundred yards in width and another of loose moraine of about the same breadth, to the margin of the glacier. While traversing the latter, perhaps a mile in width, I headed for a steep wall to the west of two snow-filled couloirs about midway along the face of the mountain.

Upon arriving at the bergschrund, I experienced some difficulty as it was open along the base of the wall which I wished to scale. This I solved by crossing it at the foot of a buttress to the right of the more westerly of the two couloirs around which I made my way by cutting steps in ice concealed by about a foot of loose snow to the rocks above the glacier. For some five hundred feet these are very precipitous, but as I had already surmounted them in scaling the highest peak, I knew that they would offer little trouble. For some distance I swung somewhat to the right, alternating between climbing the face and following a sort of wide, shallow couloir, from the end of which I clambered out onto the buttress to the left, at a point not far below the one at which on several occasions I had emerged from the couloir while on my way to the highest peak.

After going directly to the southwest for perhaps two hundred feet I zigzagged back and forth up the face along a series of rounded ledges. Above these I veered to the west in the direction of the second peak. Although a couloir led from the northeast toward its summit, direct access to it was blocked by a sheer drop of considerable height. It seemed possible, however, that the wall to the right of it could be scaled and the chute entered above the drop. Upon arriving at its base, I began to climb it, finding it negotiable, but having the feeling that a few more holds distributed here and there would be very convenient. About thirty feet up the face, after testing a rock, I began to pull myself up, but the rock began to part from the wall. With little relish for landing at the bottom of the cliff, the rock on top of me, I let go and slid down the face, the rock settling back into place as soon as it was relieved of the outward pull of my weight. Fortunately my fall was arrested within a few feet by a shelf. After scrambling up to the rock again, I shoved it down, thereby making of the place where it had rested one of the desired holds which nature had failed to provide.

After scaling the wall for some distance, I swung to the right, to a steep, narrow chimney up which I squirmed to the crest of a knife edge. This I followed for a few rods and then continued along shelves on the right wall of the couloir. These afforded interesting but only moderately difficult rock work. Having arrived at the head of the couloir, I clambered out of it with some little effort and, upon emerging, came within sight of the summit monolith only a few rods distant. The problem of scaling it was accentuated by the fact that a thunder cloud was bearing down upon the mountain from the west. As the top of a slender spire over 14,000 feet above sea level is not the most desirable location to wait out an electric storm, I made all haste to climb the former before the latter should arrive.

After changing from nailed to rubber-soled shoes, I began to scramble up the granite pinnacle, carrying with me a 100

157

foot rope. Sheer on three sides, on the fourth a steep slope led about halfway up the spire. I walked with little difficulty until my head finally was only a few feet from the summit, but there further progress was stopped by a bulge directly in front, and by the weather-polished surface of the rock. Failing to hoist myself over the protuberance, I attempted to lasso the top of the rock, but my numerous attempts proved futile. I threw one end of the rope over the summit, and after descending to the base of the spire to retrieve it, returned to my former position. After attaching one end to my waist, I looped the rope around the uppermost portion of the rock and again tied it to my waist in such a way as to prevent a fall of more than a few feet, should I happen to slip. The protruding bulge and the smooth surface rendered the short scramble a strenuous one, but eventually I pulled myself to the top of the monolith, a wedge several feet in length and one foot in width. Being in fact the slender culmination of a great pinnacle falling away precipitously on every side, it was an extremely airy perch.

I made a hasty retreat, however, as the thunder cloud was only a few minutes away. Arriving at the base of the monolith, I hurriedly took a photograph, pulled down the rope, built a small cairn, picked up my nailed shoes, and without waiting to put them on, began to drop down into the head of the couloir up which I came. Presently I was enveloped in whirling snow and rather violent wind, but the electric accompaniment did not prove so severe as I had anticipated.

Continuing along the side of the chute and over the arête, I came to the head of the chimney. In it, and on the wall below it, I used the rope considerably, but arrived at the foot without mishap. After creeping into a niche which afforded partial shelter from whirling wind and driving snow, I ate a hasty luncheon and presently was on my way again. Instead of descending the lower wall with its wet, slippery holds, I swung to the right and entered the couloir. Except for the cutting of steps for some distance in steep ice, and some maneuvering in getting across the schrund at the base of the couloir, this was accomplished without incident.

With the bergschrund safely crossed, I shot down the snow fan below it in a swift glissade. Soon the sky was clear again; with some elation I gazed upward at the topmost spire on the second highest peak of the North Palisade, attained for the first time by human effort.

158

The First Traverse of the Highest Peaks
of the North Palisade

To ME THE MOST FASCINATING of the higher peaks of the Sierra Nevada is the North Palisade, the third highest, and in some respects the finest peak in the entire range. Both from the south and north it rises in precipitous, couloir-fluted walls to a series of great spires, the loftiest of these attaining an altitude of 14,242 feet above sea level. Along its northern base lies a glacier, the largest in the Sierra.

Although the loftiest of these peaks was ascended for the first time in 1903, for upwards of a score of years it remained unscaled except by a single route, the other spires remaining unclimbed until within the past four years, and not until the past summer was a complete traverse made of the three highest ones.

On the morning of June 29 a party of three, Hervey Voge and David Brower, from Berkeley, and I set forth from our camp on the Big Pine Lakes at an elevation of some 11,000 feet above sea level with this object in view. The weather was perfectly clear and the indications were that it would remain so during the day. There was still snow along the ledges on the precipitous north face of the mountain, more than was desirable, but we could not afford to wait for it to disappear.

Upon reaching the margin of the glacier, a matter of several miles from camp, we began to traverse its gradually rising incline which increases from a few degrees along its lower margin to perhaps forty degrees as its upper margin is approached. We were aiming at a large chute about midway along the mountain, leading up to a very large V-notch between the second highest of the peaks to the left and the third highest to the right.

Nearing the upper margin of the glacier we cut steps obliquely upward across its steep grade and then made our way around a projecting buttress into the chute. Somewhat to our surprise, we found this to be free from snow. After following its floor for a short distance, we clambered up its steps on the right wall to the crest of a rib between this and another couloir. Although the crest was sufficiently broken to render a certain amount of gymnastics necessary to traverse it, and the shelves on its north side were more or less clogged with snow, we succeeded in reaching the notch without encountering any special difficulty.

To the right rose an apparently sheer and very steep face leading up toward a great blade-like peak. Up this we began to make our way, finding it not nearly so steep as it had appeared from below and provided with numerous crevices on its surface affording excellent hand- and footholds. After ascending a few hundred feet we swung to the left, traversing along ledges into a chimney. Except for some snow and a single overhang, this was only moderately difficult. Over its headwall we clambered onto the crest of the mountain.

We hastened westward along this, within a few hundred feet reaching the base of the monolith whose summit is the loftiest point, the third highest of the spires of the North Palisade, now called Thunderbolt Peak. The surmounting of this final rock, although its height is scarcely more than thirty feet, is somewhat of a problem, since it is scalable only on one side and the first eight or ten feet of that face presents little more than a roughened surface. To add to the difficulty, a deep fissure of an excellent width to break a leg in case of a fall extends along the base of the pinnacle. This vertical pitch can be negotiated by the use of a *courte echelle* or two-man stand, in which one man mounts the shoulders of another in getting a start. In this manner one of the members of the party quickly pulled himself up over the rounded projecting part of the rock and then, availing himself of the slight crevices and irregularities in the surface of the steep incline above, crawled slowly to the top of the almost blade-like monolith. He was followed by the second and then the third. After standing for some moments on the summit, we came down in succession on a doubled rope looped over the top of the rock.

Within about half an hour we were again in the notch. As the second highest point had never been scaled from the notch, the steep ascent leading up to a sharply pyramidal monolith forming the summit offered a challenge which we decided to accept. There appeared to be two possible routes, one directly up the crest, the other to the right and into a couloir, up this for a few hundred feet, and then out on its headwall to the base of the summit monolith. After some reconnoitering we decided in favor of the former.

We made our way steadily along narrow ledges and up over steep pitches, for a few hundred feet encountering nothing more than interesting rock climbing. Then we began to come upon snow, which proved rather disconcerting as we were wearing tennis shoes. Presently we were confronted by gendarme after gendarme, with deep notches between them. At times our way seemed to be blocked but always a shelf leading around the obstructing pinnacle was found.

On one occasion we were halted for some time when, the knife edge dropping away sheer on either side, advance appeared very problematic. However we found a way down over a steep drop into the next notch and thence over one steep pitch and around the shoulder of another. From here we followed a narrow ledge along a sheer wall, a drop of forty or fifty feet below it. At one point we were obliged to make a rather uncomfortably long step across a fissure. A short distance beyond this, however, upon rounding a buttress, we came to the base of a steep chimney. Although smooth and with but few handholds, this appeared to be feasible.

Up it we made our way, steadily, wedging ourselves whenever possible if sufficient holds were not available. Except for one rather dangerous handhold which was almost lost, and a long step across a gap, the top of the chimney was gained without incurring any special hazard. Above this we hastened along over steep but well-broken pitches to the base of the final monolith.

A pyramid some thirty feet in height, this monolith at first appears unscalable. In fact, it is so on three sides. However, up the steep incline on its fourth side, since the surface of the granite is rather rough, one can walk to within a few feet of the top. There a large protuberance strikes one in the chest, apparently barring further progress. It is decidedly not the place for anyone with poor nerves or superfluous *embonpoint*. It is possible for one to reach over the rounded edge of the top, and a single, rather indifferent foothold can be had far up to the right. Then by pawing with the hands and shoving at a rather awkward angle with the foot, one can work gradually over the hump to the top, a somewhat rounded area several feet long and half as much in width, more than 14,000 feet above the sea.

After the three of us had surmounted this aerial perch and roped down its vertical east face, we decided to go on to the highest peak even though it was growing late. Down a rather steep chimney we made our way to a notch, and then spiraled around an obstructing tower to a notch beyond it. We encountered difficulty there, a wide fissure and a quantity of snow just where it was most in the way. However, after some maneuvering, we succeeded in getting across the crevice. We then wedged our way up a steep incline to a wide slanting ledge which we followed for some distance. This, however, narrowed to a width of several feet, not difficult to traverse except that it was cluttered with loose rock and had a drop of hundreds of feet below.

We kicked off a goodly number of rocks which went crashing down the mountainside and then, carefully edging along the shelf, we reached the foot of a short chimney. Up this we hoisted ourselves over an overhang and then around an elbow, and finally over a steep pitch to the top of the mountain, 14,242 feet in altitude. From this superb vantage point, one of the finest in the Sierra, we looked southward fifty miles or more along the crest of the range to Mt. Whitney and about as far northwestward to the Ritter and Lyell groups of the Yosemite region. The sun being already low, we began the descent, dropping down over the great blocks of granite and steep pitches east of the top of the mountain and continuing eastward along the narrow crest.

Within a quarter of a mile we were momentarily brought to a halt at the head of a precipitous chimney leading down to a great notch several hundred feet below. Down this we carefully made our way to the notch, from which a large chute descends the north face of the mountain. Except for a tongue of rock a few hundred feet in length projecting downward from the notch, the floor of the chute was covered with ice and snow.

We followed this tongue to its lower end and then began to descend the snow, which was inclined at an angle of about forty-five degrees. For some distance we were able to kick into it, but then it became a matter of patiently cutting steps down its frozen surface. At the lower end of the couloir and immediately above the glacier we came upon an ice wall. A line of steps cut obliquely down its face allowed us to descend it and, with this, the arduous climb was over.

Shadows lay across the glacier, its freezing surface crunched beneath the impact of our nailed boots, but the light of the declining sun fell athwart the jagged summits of the North Palisade. Presently it assumed an amber hue which soon deepened to a vivid rose. This, in turn, faded and the mountains became enveloped in the darkness of night.

162

The Rosy Finch of the Sierra Nevada

In THE ARCTIC-ALPINE ZONE of the Sierra Nevada, extending from timberline—an average elevation in the Sierra of perhaps 10,500 feet—to the summits of the highest peaks more than 14,000 feet above the sea, there is a scattering of bird life. It is most abundant in autumn both because birds resident in that zone during the summer have by then reared their broods and because birds usually found at lower elevations stray upward into these apparently inhospitable areas. This may be in part a response to wandering propensities which seem to induce individuals, both birds and mammals, to roam beyond the limits of their usual habitat. Most of them are, however, doubtless lured thither by the relative abundance of food above timberline in autumn. Insects are much more numerous than would be supposed by persons unfamiliar with these high elevations. There are also the seeds and berries of small alpine plants, shrubs which survive at an elevation of more than 12,000 feet, and small herbs which are sometimes observed above 14,000.

On a number of occasions I have come upon grouse a considerable distance above timberline, feeding upon these, and once at an elevation of some 12,000 feet I saw a covey of valley quail. During this season also, for no very obvious reason, the Clark nutcracker has the habit of straying upward, sometimes even to the summits of the highest peaks. A scattering of hawks is also present. In late spring and early summer the mountaineer occasionally hears the jubilant song of the rock wren and even in late autumn he may observe it darting in and out among the rocks.

In spring, summer and autumn, seldom does the mountaineer scale any of the higher peaks of the Sierra without encountering the rosy finch, sometimes singly, but in summer more often in pairs, and in autumn in broods or in flocks of considerable size. They appear to hover and linger about the highest peaks for the mere pleasure of doing so. They usually flit about from rock to rock, uttering a pleasing "churring" sound, for the rosy finch does not appear to have what might properly be called a song. They will come within a few feet of the visitor to what they probably regard as their special domain, possibly to extend greetings. The rosy finch is in fact one of the most confiding small birds, partly from natural disposition but doubtless also from the fact that its habitat is beyond that of *homo sapiens.* It has had no unpleasant experiences with this featherless biped, and, not sensing in him a natural enemy, sees no reason to suspect harm.

If a camp be established during summer near timberline the rosy finch is likely to become a frequent visitor, spending considerable time picking up crumbs. I remember a case of this kind at a trail camp on Mt. Whitney at an elevation of 13,500 feet. Early in the season the rosy finches formed the habit of visiting the camp. Later they appeared, bringing along their half-grown broods. These became so tame that we could approach within several feet of them without their becoming alarmed. In summer rosy finches linger about the summit of Mt. Whitney, picking up fragments of food discarded by mountain climbers.

The rosy finch builds its nest in places so inaccessible that very few of them have been found. Usually they are in a cleft or crevice on the face of a cliff, although, if I remember correctly, I once discovered one under a large rock on a stretch of talus. Earlier I had discovered one merely by accident. As I was sliding along a ledge on the face of an unnamed mountain near Mt. Whitney, a small bird flew out from a crevice, its wings almost brushing my face. A glance around revealed to me a rosy finch and its nest in the narrow crevice several feet distant.

Haunting the higher mountains during most of the year, the rosy finch does not appear to have numerous enemies. The Clark crow is said to be its archenemy, but in ten years of roaming the Sierra Nevada, I have seen no evidence for this. The pigeon hawk, which is sometimes seen in localities frequented by the rosy finch, in all likelihood preys in some measure upon them. Probably also a prowling marten or a weasel occasionally pounces upon an unsuspecting rosy finch.

In autumn the rosy finch tends to collect in rather large flocks which stay together throughout the winter. Although at times rosy finches may be seen at lofty elevations even in midwinter, as deep snow covers the high mountains they descend to moderately low elevations. There they frequent slopes and ridges where the wind has withered herbs on the seeds of which the rosy finch subsists. When spring arrives, however, the flocks of rosy finches break up. The mountaineer who ascends the high peaks in April and May will almost always see rosy finches flying about. Soon they mate and the year's cycle begins again.

Punctuality and the programming of his time are charac-
teristic traits in spite of the fact that one may find him spending
the entire afternoon in the outdoor parlor of his old cabin, or
sleeping late in the equally outdoor bedroom. Sleeping late
would mean being in bed—on the ancient couch covered with
ragged tarpaulin under the locust tree, where Norman slumbers
the night for ten months of the year as a respite from claustro-
phobia of the house—until after the summer sunrise. But you
can bet he has his arising time planned, and the afternoon talk
or all-morning reading session is also part of the program.

He is perhaps as he has been described; the old-fashioned
gentleman, with maybe a little bit of victorianism or even a bit
of puritanism unwittingly seeping from that minister's son back-
ground of many years ago. Probably he would have to be labeled
a conservative, at least in most senses of the word not imme-
diately connected with politics. It may be that he reads and ap-
preciates Thoreau, but it is easy for an awed young Clyde ad-
mirer to get carried away and compare him with Vinobe Bhave,
the walking saint of India, when a more apt example might be
Kit Carson. When he comes to our house nowadays, he may sit
in the straight-backed chair by the window, with his old cam-
paign hat on to shade his good eye from the overhead light, and
read for most of the day and into the evening, stopping only for
his three squares and a snooze and a bit of a blast now and then
at something. If a book is on the davenport he will pick it up,
and if the title reads anything like The Awakening of Faith in
the Mahayana *or* The Affluent Society *or* God and Man at Yale,
he drops it instantly and heaves to his feet to follow the well-
worn path to the section of our bookcase where his thumbprints
mark Some Problems of Pleistocene Morphology, Land and
Land Forms, Life on the Arctic Slope, *etc.*

One time he got hold of a book on a couple who had spent
some winters in the Brooks Range of Alaska. He got a lot of
mileage out of that one. For a couple of years he found a way
to work anecdotes from this book—I think there must have been
a series of books—into almost every conversation. He never
could remember names, or doesn't try to, but anyway, just as he
nicknames almost every one he meets, he immediately captioned
the authors of these books. He always referred to them as the
"Eat-a-Mooses." Apparently they ate a moose a day, and after
the nickname and explanation, he would launch into a long dis-
cussion on their particular methods of wilderness survival.

166

About half the time he would be granting a grudging approval of their techniques, and then he'd think of something which touched one of the numerous, exposed nerves in the body of gospel of how-to-go-out-and-live-in-the-woods-with-only-a-gun-and-a-bag-of-salt-according-to-Norman-Clyde, and wham! Just like a sonic boom he would blast us out of our complacent non-hearing of the dull monologue with loud and pithy profanity. But just for a few seconds, for the chuckle is always close upon the curse, and then he would be off on a theme of his own, a long-winded story of what happened in that canyon over on the other side of Mount . . .

It seems to me you told me over the telephone not to philosophize about Norman, or eulogize him, and that you did not want an essay on what a noble specimen he was and what a great contribution to literature on the mystique of the outdoors, and on what he meant to the cosmos and vice versa, and all that crap. Well, I apologize if I have sometimes gotten close to what you did not want. I know you wanted a string of anecdotes of trips with Norman in the mountains, and although I'm sure there must have been a book's worth of these had I the sense to have written them down, I just cannot think of many now. Therefore, I have tried to describe what he was like and, more particularly, because of my short memory, what he has been like recently and what he is like at the present moment. Also, I wanted to try to use my rather frequent and somewhat more intimate acquaintance than most people have had with Norman to try to get a little bit inside him to see what kind of a man he is.

Of course, while Norman is almost garrulous on some occasions and for some subjects, he is extremely reticent when it comes to anything personal, and this is where observers go wrong in trying to assess his character. Neither Jules—his intimate companion on a long list of the early thirties first ascents —nor I had ever suspected that Norman had been married. It is an interesting comment that Wheelock obtained this information simply by asking Norman. Anyhow, Norman does carry a certain reserve and he obviously does not want to discuss his private life, and if one gets to prying so much as to ask his age, he will pointedly suggest that it is none of anybody's business. I don't really know him. Who does? Does anybody really know anybody? Actually, Norman has been for so long a permanent fixture of the landscape of our lives here that he has become like an old uncle, who is sometimes a trial and often a pride, but normally an integral part of the scene, whose wrinkled contours of eccentricity, familiarity or inscrutability are no more to be noted or analyzed than the cragged face of the mountain outside my window.

Well, I've been dogging off quite a bit since you called a couple of months ago, and have only the excuse that I've been down with a bad back and a bum hip much of the time. We plan to go to Big Pine to check on Norman again, so I'll knock this off for now and hope that all this rambling garbage contains some nuggets you may be able to use, Dave. Sure wish I had kept notes all these years. Also apologize again for so much personal stuff, but that's the only way I could think of to write it and anyway, you are going to edit the hell out of it, I hope.

Yours,

Smoke

Epilogue

WITHOUT EXAGGERATION it can be said that Norman has waited ten years for this book, because it was about 1961 that he signed a contract with a publisher. They never saw eye to eye on what kind of a book it was to be, and Norman expressed very well, I suspect, what the discrepancy was in a letter of September, 1964, to Francis Farquhar: " . . . As to writing, during the past several years I have done a considerable amount of it—enough for at least two 350-page books—as far as quantity goes. Several years ago Prentice Hall of New York, wangled me into signing a contract to write a book, which they insisted on calling an autobiography, although I told them plainly that I did not know of any subject on which I was less interested in writing than on myself, and added that outside of my mountain and wilderness experiences I had never done much that was in any way remarkable."

In the same letter Norman goes on to mention the contract provision for calling in another writer (if necessary) at $3,000 —to be taken out of royalties—and further, that he was quite sure what the publisher really wanted was a "hopped up personal story."

Along about 1965 Norman and David Brower, then of the Sierra Club, began to get together on the proposed book, and a great deal of fine work was done on the project, notably by Fred Fertig, Bruce Kilgore, Bob Golden, Dan Gridley, and Tom Turner. But the book got caught in the Club's Armageddon and sank quietly out of sight behind the front lines. And so, in April 1970, at the insistence of Smoke Blanchard and Jules Eichorn, I journeyed to Big Pine and there, with Jules, met Norman for the first time—at Baker Creek Ranch.

It was spring in the foothills of the Sierra, and later than spring at the Ranch. Norman came outside when we yelled, and the three of us sat in the outdoor living room for at least two hours. The whole thing was unforgettable. Baker Creek Ranch had been Norman's home since the early fifties, and he had planted many of the vines that were all over everything; an offshoot of the Creek ran next to the house, there were lizards under

169

every twig, the air was perfumed, there was Norman's huge wickiup for sleeping under the early-winter southwest wind off the peaks—not an ordinary brush wickiup, but one made of poles ten feet long and seven inches in diameter, there were the outbuildings of deep brown planks and the old corral, the cottonwoods, the inscrutable ranch house stocked with fifty years of you-name-it, as Smoke Blanchard has written (we did not go inside)—and most of all there was the Old Gaffer sitting with us in the outdoor living room underneath the ever-present campaign hat, reminiscing about high Sierra rambles of long ago.

Norman's heart was good on the subject of the book for which he was still waiting, and we agreed he would dig out some typescripts the next morning. Finally the three of us walked down the two-track road for the gate and the car and Bishop and the Blanchard house for the night. I went ahead so I could get a photograph of the two whose climbing friendship went back forty years—Eichorn and Clyde. Up behind them as they sauntered through the late spring light were the foothills of Norman's mountains, beyond the cottonwoods—veiled by the afternoon haze.

The next morning Norman and I went back to the Ranch and he quickly disappeared into his house, to return with a grocery box full of manuscripts. He set the box in the sun and sat himself down on the dirt and started sorting. Within a half hour there were four boxes worth of manuscripts all over the ground, but Norman was finding what he wanted for, after all, to each his own on a filing system. By then there had been too many unforgettable scenes in less than twenty-four hours, and although I took a few photographs of the proceedings, I mostly hunkered down and watched. Smoke Blanchard has described Norman as dignified, aloof, reserved, and Smoke is quite correct. But there was nothing reserved about the way Norman attacked that pile of writings. They were his old friends and he knew all of them well and he knew which ones he wanted to give me.

Shortly before noon the unforgettable scene ended and Norman and I shook hands. There was going to be a book, and it was going to be Norman's book almost entirely, but we agreed there had to be something written *about* him, though not much.

Collection of the Clyde materials from the Sierra Club took five months following the meeting with Norman, and I am greatly indebted to August Frugé and Ted Wilentz for agreeing immediately to release the work so my search could begin, and

170

to Barbara Brower and Dan Rosenberg for leading me to the last items, namely the field journals and the bulk of Norman's original typescripts. Then, in order to keep things rolling on this ten-year book, I asked Mary Millman to read Norman's work and select and sequence the essays. When the two of them met in Berkeley in May, 1971, Norman got started on some stories and it was difficult to pry him away from Mary's company.

At this point some words of explanation are needed, I think. There will be some, or perhaps many, who will feel this book should have included extensive biographical information on Norman, plus a complete bibliography of magazine articles Norman placed over the years, plus a list of his numerous first ascents in the Sierra, a list of his climbs in Canada, Montana, Idaho, Colorado, the Cascades, and so on. But Walt Wheelock, in *Close Ups of the High Sierra* (La Siesta Press, Box 406, Glendale, California, 1962; second printing 1966, *in print* at $2.50 paperbound) has covered much of that, and it seemed absurd to repeat what Walt had done. Further, Norman has no use for biographical fact (which he feels becomes slightly fictionized whenever he is interviewed for a magazine or newspaper article), and further, he and I had an implicit agreement on the matter.

So the biographical skeleton of fact will be mentioned here, and no more. Norman came out of Philadelphia, and by the time he was five was wandering with his sister all over the western Pennsylvania and Ohio farmlands and patches of hardwood forest. His family moved to Canada when he was twelve, eighty miles from Ottawa. By the time he was sixteen he had learned woodsmanship from the Highland Scots settled in the area, especially handling of the axe and the crosscut saw, and on the farms, the bucksaw. Norman was seventeen when his father died, and the family moved back to the eastern United States. He took a factory job for awhile and loathed it, then enrolled at Geneva College and graduated in 1909. He reached California in 1910 or 1911, having been strongly influenced by the writings of John Muir, especially *The Mountains of California.*

About 1911 Norman married, in southern California, and lived with his wife for one year, during which they took one or two camping trips into the San Gabriels. Tuberculosis forced her to a sanitarium, where she died two years later.

Norman's first summer in the Sierra was 1914, beginning an association which would span more than fifty-five years. He

171

spent some twenty winters at Glacier Lodge on Big Pine Creek, and almost that many winters at Baker Creek Ranch. And the peaks. What of the high places? Norman loves every bump in the Sierra, and most of the animals and all the trees. But sitting on the ground at Fourth Recess in August, 1970, he allowed that the North Palisade was his favorite, and that he had climbed it at least thirty-five times. He was looking up at the heights as he said this, and I could see the glint in his eye.

As for Norman's essays, they go back into the late twenties, although the majority were written in the thirties, forties, and fifties. A few of those reproduced here appeared thirty and forty years ago—usually under somewhat different title and in a different form—in *Touring Topics* (subsequently *Westways*), *Motorland, National Motorist, American Alpine Journal,* and *Sierra Club Bulletin.*

On April 8th next, Norman will have a birthday. He will be eighty-seven and, according to himself, he is therefore a holdover from the Eocene. I thought of this as we sat once again in the outdoor living room at Baker Creek Ranch in mid-October, 1971. The ranch house had been looted and totally vandalized by the local hoodlums while Norman was staying in Big Pine, and Norman knew he could never live there again. All the vines he had planted were dead because others had diverted the water, and Norman was telling Jules it was the end of an era—the end of his Baker Creek Ranch home.

It was another of those unforgettable scenes, as the Old Gaffer sat there, a high-mountain holdover from the Eocene underneath his campaign hat. And both of his long-time friends—Jules Eichorn and Smoke Blanchard—called it. Norman was absolutely in tune with his environment and he was never just passing through. He lived among the peaks, beyond the cottonwoods and above the haze. As near as I can tell, he's still up there.

DAVE BOHN
Berkeley
October 1971

172

Three thousand copies of Norman's book were printed by Noel Young Press, Santa Barbara, in November, 1971. Composition and title page design by Graham Mackintosh. Mary Millman selected and edited the Clyde essays. The frontispiece, second section of photographs, and design by Dave Bohn.
The East Face of Mt. Whitney from Mt. Russell is from a Norman Clyde negative. Five hundred copies handbound by Earle Gray, Los Angeles.

The 1927 Chevrolet, Baker Creek Ranch, 1956.
Photograph by Smoke Blanchard.